Enjoy!
Sandra
5 Apr 22

D1297521

- LIFE IS A JOURNEY - LIFE IS A JOURNEY - LIFE IS A JOURNEY - STOCKTON

480
Codorus Street

Surviving Unpredictability

SANDRA L. KEARSE-STOCKTON

BALBOA.PRESS
A DIVISION OF HAY HOUSE

This book is a work of non-fiction. Unless otherwise noted, the author and the publisher make no explicit guarantees as to the accuracy of the information contained in this book and in some cases, names of people and places have been altered to protect their privacy.

Balboa Press books may be ordered through booksellers or by contacting:

Balboa Press
A Division of Hay House
1663 Liberty Drive
Bloomington, IN 47403
www.balboapress.com
844-682-1282

Because of the dynamic nature of the Internet, any web addresses or links contained in this book may have changed since publication and may no longer be valid. The views expressed in this work are solely those of the author and do not necessarily reflect the views of the publisher, and the publisher hereby disclaims any responsibility for them.

The author of this book does not dispense medical advice or prescribe the use of any technique as a form of treatment for physical, emotional, or medical problems without the advice of a physician, either directly or indirectly. The intent of the author is only to offer information of a general nature to help you in your quest for emotional and spiritual well-being. In the event you use any of the information in this book for yourself, which is your constitutional right, the author and the publisher assume no responsibility for your actions.

Any people depicted in stock imagery provided by Getty Images are models, and such images are being used for illustrative purposes only. Certain stock imagery © Getty Images.

Interior Image Credit: Karmentrina Schevelle Kearse

Print information available on the last page.

ISBN: 978-1-9822-5557-2 (sc)
ISBN: 978-1-9822-5556-5 (hc)
ISBN: 978-1-9822-5317-2 (e)

Library of Congress Control Number: 2020918547

Balboa Press rev. date: 10/01/2020

Dedication and Foreword

This book is dedicated to all of the women and men with or without children trying to survive life, as we know it, in this world today. Giving a special shout-out to the following persons.

My sister, Mary Elizabeth Smallwood-Richardson

My sister, Mabel Lee Smallwood-Reid

My sister, Dorothy Mae Smallwood-Stewart (Rest in Peace, my sister)

My sister, Lugenia Smallwood-(Mitchell) Washington

My sister, Bonita Faith Smallwood (Banks) Swann

My brother, Clifford Earl (Bucky) Smallwood (Rest in Peace, my brother)

My daughter, Kimmy Jo Kearse

My son, Kevin Scott Kearse Senior

My daughter, Karmentrina Schevelle Kearse

My son, Keenan Wynn Kearse, Sr. (Rest in Peace, my son)

A host of grandchildren, great grandchildren, foster children, cousins, nephews, nieces, aunts, uncles, friends, and colleagues.

<u>*Abundant Living*</u>

Anonymous author from the book of "Shared Treasures," compiled by

Roseline J. Young.

Think deeply,

Speak gently

Laugh Often

Work Hard

Give Freely

Pay Promptly

Pray Earnestly

Be kind always

Foreword

IN 1999, I TRANSFERRED TO the U.S. Army Reserve Hospital located at Walter Reed Army Hospital in Washington, D.C. It was there that I met Lieutenant Colonel (LTC) Sandra "Sandi" Stockton. She was quite engaging as we chatted about our lives, families, children, careers, etc. We were both LTCs and connected easily. I found her to be very smart and strong. I remember feeling shocked when she mentioned that she had lost two close family members in a house fire just years before. Her eyes welled with tears that streamed down her face. I was stunned by the enormity of her loss and thrown off to see this strong officer present such a vulnerable side. And although I offered condolences and support, it felt inadequate at best. I felt a bond with her for trusting and sharing that part of her life with me so readily.

LTC Stockton shared many positives about her life as well. She shared that she and her husband had several children and foster children. I remember thinking that, as a drilling reservist, this lady had a lot on her plate. I wondered how she juggled so much responsibility. She seemed to have it all, and lots of it. My life seemed so simple in comparison.

Over the next several years, I had minimal contact with her; we worked in different sections of the unit. In 2003, I became Chief Nurse, and came to rely on LTC Stockton as a dependable go-to person, whether it was to fill in as the Officer in Charge, the need to mentor new lieutenants, or to provide discipline, not that I had to ask. She always stepped up.

One vivid memory of LTC Stockton was her leadership as the Officer in Charge during an Annual Training Period at Fort McCoy, Wisconsin, in 2005. Her incredible organizational and people skills endeared her to the troops. The training was a huge success. Not only did she demonstrate superior leadership, Soldiers reported it was "one of the best-ever summer camps."

Only months later, I was called to active duty. I hand-picked LTC Stockton to take over the Chief Nurse position trusting that she had the strength, professionalism, and the knowledge to perform the job. She declined but agreed to step in until replaced. A decision I could only respect.

Shortly after that, I learned that we had numerous delinquent Officer Evaluation Reports. Again, knowing her work ethic, I reached out to LTC Stockton for assistance. She orchestrated and executed an entire project to complete the reports, a monumental task that involved a team of officers. When the new Commander arrived in January 2006, all evaluation reports were completed. I am still grateful to her. I could never have done it without her.

In April 2007, I learned that LTC Stockton had lost another close family member. I perceived the loss to be unbearable, especially for someone who had already suffered extreme losses. I attended the repast but was at a loss for words. I do not know how she summoned the strength to continue.

When I returned from active duty in 2008, LTC Stockton had left the unit. I missed seeing her at drills, but we managed to keep in touch. Over the years, I have come to consider her as one of the most resilient women I have ever known. Her survival of extreme losses of several family members is a testament to her remarkable ability to hold on. Her psychological toughness and strength of character confirm her ability to endure and to grow from adversity.

Amazingly, Sandra Stockton loves and lives life to the fullest; she perseveres and grows despite huge obstacles. It was notable to me that she had also put herself through undergraduate and graduate schools while working outside her home and caring for her family.

This book is for everyone but especially for people who find themselves struggling against the odds. It is a guide for those navigating their journeys and dreams for a better life. When people think they have the hardest time and cannot find their way out of turmoil, I encourage reading this book for inspiration, guidance, and perspective. There is consolation in knowing that someone else had an insurmountable struggle and who not only succeeded, but also triumphed. LTC Stockton found her niche in helping others. This book illustrates her journey, her struggles, and successes to victory.

It has been my sincere honor to contribute the foreword to 480 Codorus Street. Sandi Stockton is such an amazing and phenomenal woman. It is my belief that readers will gain perspective and encouragement from this book. I have the greatest admiration for Sandi, and I am proud to call her my friend.

Sharon A. Singleton, COL (Retired)
U.S. Army Reserve

Introduction

EVERYTHING THAT YOU READ HERE is from my memories, from my perspective only. Although my siblings have experienced many of the same things that I have experienced, their perspective might be very different. We were all cut from the same cloth, but all very different. With that, allow me to introduce you to my family and me.

Welcome to the life of Sandra Lee Smallwood. I was born June 14, 1949 at York Hospital, York, Pennsylvania at 2:50 in the morning on Flag Day. My nickname is "Lou," given to me later on by mom, Dot. It was a windy, cloudy day with a temperature of 77 degrees Fahrenheit. My parents, Dorothy Mae Jackson Smallwood (Dot) and William Junior Smallwood, were adding me to their family of three. I had an older sister already at home, Mary Elizabeth, who was eighteen months old. Dot and I had to stay in the hospital for three days since that was the hospital policy. (In the early days, we called our parents by their first names. We never questioned it. It was just our way of life.) It allowed time for the two of us to become acquainted. One could say it was the beginning of an unbreakable bond between Dot and me. They say that we choose our parents before birth. I certainly chose Dot. I have always felt close to her, and imagine the bonding started in the hospital bed, which eventually led to us being lifelong friends.

It was soon time for Dot and William to take me home to meet Mary Elizabeth. Our home at 480 Codorus Street was a beautiful, red-brick detached home with a large concrete front porch. We walked through a vestibule to get to the inside of the rest of the house, followed by the living room. It was enormous and open, with a huge front window that faced the street. The next room was the dining room with a small potbelly coal stove, a dining room table with six chairs and a china cabinet with lots of pretty trinkets and glass dishes. There was also a sizable, tall window in the left corner of the room. That window gave a view of the concrete side of the gigantic backyard. The kitchen was enormous with a big wooden table; it looked like an army could fit at that table. We also had a very large coal and wood-burning stove and a fridge that had to have dry ice inside to keep food cold. At the back of the house, there was a spacious wooden back porch with railings around it. There was also a small closed in corner outhouse. The outhouse had a toilet that flushed. There was no heat in that room and no running hot water, only cold water. Therefore, in the winter, you did not want to stay in there too long. It was dark; one would have to feel around for the string coming from the ceiling and pull it to get the light on. It was scary in there, and at any given moment, a rat could show up.

To get to the yard, we had to walk down a few steps from the porch. Our backyard was spacious with a big tree that our dog's chain wrapped around to tether him. Our dog's name was Rex. My spirit was already in that house. I could feel that I had visited there before my birth. William and Dot continued to add to the family.

William was hoping for a boy, but girls just kept on coming. Mabel Lee (no nickname) came to join us on July of 1950; Dorothy Mae (Dottie Mae) joined us July 1951. Lugenia joined the crew in Aug of 1952 (nicknamed Pokey). Bonita Faith came on board in June of 1954, (nicknamed Nee Nee), and finally a little brother in September of 1955,

Clifford Earl, (nicknamed Bucky.) Mary had no nickname. By the way, Dot gave me my nickname because It reminded her of the cartoon little girl on television, Little Lulu. She said I was always getting into something like her.

Chapter 1

Our Connection to the World

I REALLY DO BELIEVE THAT OUR given names influence our lives tremendously, as well as our personalities. Your name is the greatest connection to your own identity and individuality. On the other hand, our physical traits determine how others initially perceive us. Our character weighs heavily on our internal factors, like our personality and self-perception. I also think that it matters what names we give our children. For instance, my father named me after one his first cousin's daughters who lived in Orangeburg, South Carolina. My younger sister, Lugenia, he named after his sister and Mabel after his mother, Mabel Paul-Smallwood. My mother named my sister Mary Elizabeth after her mother's middle name. Her name was Margaret Elizabeth Ryan. My younger sister Dottie Mae was her namesake, Dorothy Mae, as my mother after her aunt. My baby sister, Bonita Faith, was lucky. Bonita had her own original name and did not have to live up to anyone in the family. My baby brother, Clifford Earl came last and mom named him after her brother Clifford. William was quite happy about the birth of Clifford. He now had a son, something he wanted more than anything he ever did.

William loved his fair-skinned children, Mary and Bonita, or maybe it was the blonde hair. Bonita and I were very close in color but for some reason I was never his pick. He absolutely loved Clifford (Bucky), as we all did. Bucky could have had green skin and it would not have mattered, the luck of being the only boy. He did not show very much love towards Mabel and Lugenia because he considered them too dark. Dottie Mae wore the burden of being born to light. William denied Dottie Mae at birth because he said she looked like the white milkman's baby (William's words exactly). She was damn near white! My siblings and I cut from the same cloth but are truly different. I guess William did not understand Dot's ancestral color spectrum or his. Dot's grandmother was mulatto. She was Irish and her family immigrated to the Confederate States of America in the 1800s. Dot's grandfather was the son of a freed slave from Virginia. William's grandmother was Cherokee and Black. That speaks for the blended colors bestowed upon us.

Mary Elizabeth was born in January under the zodiac sign of Aquarius. Aquarius and Scorpio signs are supposed to be the smartest of the zodiac signs. Mom always said as we grew up that Mary Elizabeth was her smartest child. Bonita and I were born in June under the zodiac sign of Gemini. Gemini is the craziest, unpredictable, sporadic, and most volatile personality out of all the zodiac signs. Mabel was born in July under sign of Cancer. Cancer is one of the five zodiac signs that appear shy but are not really; they think before they talk. Mabel always sucked her thumb, especially if she was worried about something. I called her out on it many times, but she denied it every time. Dorothy Mae was born in July and Lugenia was born in August -- both fall under the sign of Leo. Leos are optimistic, passionate, and spontaneous. Clifford Earl was born in September under the sign of Libra. Libras adore high art, intellectualism, and connoisseurship. Our mother was a Sagittarius, optimistic, restless, progressive, and adventurous. They cannot stand to be contained. Father was a Capricorn; they are detail-oriented, perseverance in getting what they want. As a child, I knew nothing of the zodiac signs but now that I am older, I understand how they influenced the lives of me and my family.

Chapter 2

480 Codorus Street, York, Pennsylvania Living in a Bubble

D OT AND WILLIAM NOW HAD a full house. We always called our mom Dot and our dad William. I do not know why but we always did. Not too long ago, I reached out to one of my first cousins, Shirley Miller-Thompkins and spoke with her about it because she and her siblings called their mom and dad by their first names, Sis and Beef. When talking to other first cousins, they did not call their parents by their first name. I have no reason why. My siblings and I knew they were mom and dad.

Dot was a homemaker and William was a long-haul truck driver, which kept him away from home most of the time. There were good times when William was not at home. We were all growing up pretty fast. At the age of three in 1952, I began attending preschool at Chrispus Attucks Center. Mary started twelve months ahead of me. I cried, kicked, screamed, and pulled Dot's skirt as hard as I could for a three-year-old, but she and the teacher separated us. Dot left me there with my sister and a whole lot of strange people. I was wondering how in the world she could leave her baby girl there with all those kids. My sister,

Mary, was hugging me and telling me not to cry, wiping my eyes with her shirt. She would not leave me. We hung on to each other all day and for several more days to come. I finally accepted that Dot was going to keep taking me to that place with Mary. Therefore, I just settled down and accepted it. She was always there to pick us up on time with her big, gray buggy with four big wheels. One wheel squeaked all the time. Dot kept complaining about it every time we were in it. She was always worried that the squeaky back wheel would fall off. Dot would push us way across town to our house at 480 Codorus Street. She would stop at Penn Park on the way home because she would get tired from pushing the buggy. We loved it because we played on the merry-go-round, took our shoes off, and played in the sandbox. We did not want to leave the park but Dot said it was time to go home. She would pack us up for the walk across the long wooden College Avenue Bridge to 480 Codorus Street. Neighbors would be waving and yelling to her, "How are you doing?" Dot would yell back, "I am okay."

We all took our turns going to preschool. Mabel did not join us because of a heart condition and was in and out of Heart Haven Hospital in Lancaster, Pennsylvania with her rheumatic heart condition. By that time, Dottie Mae and Lugenia were in preschool and Mary and I had moved up to Princess Street School and Lincoln Elementary school. We were all still getting rides in Dot's big gray buggy when she had to go to the local store to buy items that she needed for the house. She would walk to Charlie Myers' Store where she had store credit. If we were quiet, we would get a piece of penny candy.

September 1954, Mary was now six years old and did not have to go to preschool anymore. She had to go to a real kindergarten school without me. She cried, screamed, kicked, and used all of her strength to hold on to Dot's skirt. It did not work; she was going into that school no matter what she did. With Dot and William, we were a family of eight,

5

and Dot really needed a break from cleaning our big house, taking care of six children, sometimes with a baby on the way; it was a bit much for her, and she had to do everything all alone. Since William was rarely home, Dot decided that Mary and I were all old enough to do some work around the house.

Housework consisted of filling up buckets with coal and then carrying it from the cellar to the kitchen and dining room coal stoves. The loads of coal were small and that was no problem. We had to make several trips, so Dot did not have to climb the stairs. We also helped her out with carrying wet laundry to the yard and holding the clothespin bag while she hung the laundry. Dot used a washing board to wash all of our clothing until William purchased her an electric washing machine. Dot would fill up a big tin round tub on the kitchen floor and sit on a chair to scrub the clothes up and down on the wash board until they were clean. After our chores, we could play out in our backyard with our little sisters. Our yard was huge, full of dirt and trees. We did not need any friends at that time. We had our own backyard playground activities. We jumped rope, made mud pies, roller-skated, and played Cowboys and Indians. Dot did not worry about anyone bothering us in the backyard because we had our big dog, Rex, on a very long chain tied to the big tree right beside our wooden back porch. We barely knew there were any other children around.

When Mabel came home for visits from the hospital, she would tell us all about the nurses and doctors at the hospital. Mabel had all kinds of ideas for us to have fun. She always chose what we would play when she was home. We would listen to her because she was sickly, and we did not want her to get upset because she said her heart would burst open and she would die. We did not want Mabel to die. We were somewhat jealous of Mabel when it was time to go back to the hospital, and we all wanted a turn to go with her to the hospital.

One day when Dot was using her electric washing machine, Mabel and I thought we would help her. We watched her take the wet clothes out of the washer tub and put them through the ringer. While she went to the kitchen to check the food on the stove, Mabel and I took a towel out of the tub of water to put it through the ringer. Mabel did not move her hand fast enough and her fingers started going through the ringer. She started screaming and I started calling Dot. Dot ran into the washroom as fast as she could. At that time, Dot was pregnant.

Dot started trying to stop the ringer from going around. She was banging on the ringer with a hammer and it just would not open. Finally, it dawned on her to pull the plug out of the wall socket. Dot wrapped Mabel's bent-up arm and sent Mary to Miss Isabelle's house around the corner to get help. Someone came and drove Dot and Mabel to the York Hospital Emergency Room. Mabel came home with a cast up her entire arm. We all wrote our names on her cast. I was sure glad William was not at home; it would have been my entire fault because I was older than Mabel was. Mabel really played the poor sick child part during that time. Lord knows she was already good at it. Dot made her stay in the house for a while with her casted arm. I stayed in and kept her company most of the time. Another time, she talked me into trading my teenage doll with her teenage doll. Mabel decided one day to cut off all the hair off my doll and then wanted her doll back. I refused. She went to Dot, crying, "Lou will not give me my doll back." Dot came and saw my doll was bald. I was still holding her doll and crying. Dot told me to give Mabel her doll. Now I was crying very hard because I did not want my doll back with a bald head. Dot told me she would get me a brand-new doll, and she did get me one later. I learned then that I could not trust Mabel with my toys because she was surely an Indian giver.

We would have stone throwing battles with the Gilbert boys who lived a few houses from us. A rock was flying and hit me in the back of my head. Blood was everywhere. My siblings, as always, yelled for Dot. A neighbor took us to the hospital. Some neighbor was always willing to take Dot to the hospital for emergencies with her kids. Once again, we visited the York Hospital emergency room, where I received several sutures in my head. The nurse told me that if I was strong and did not cry, she would give me some candy. I cried a little when injected with the numbing medicine; after that, it was a piece a cake. The nurse gave me enough lollipops for my siblings and me.

A few days passed, and Mabel was home for another visit. Of course, that meant that whatever we played had to have Mabel's stamp of approval. A favorite game of Mabel's was cowboys and Indians, so one day we were playing, and Mabel decided that we needed an Indian to hang from the tree that stood over our large back porch. We agreed.

"Mabel asked, "Who wants to be the Indian?"

Our sister Pokey, raised her hand shouting, "I will, I will."

Mabel took down one of Dots clotheslines, and I went into the house and got a chair. Mabel tied one end of the line to a large branch on the tree and the other end around Pokey's neck. She then told Pokey to step up on a chair; Mabel, Dottie Mae, and I helped Pokey to get up on chair because she was only four years old, and she could not climb up on the chair herself. Mabel put the rope around her neck and told Pokey she had to kick and scream like on television when she pushed her off the chair. We had a television set, so we knew what the Indian was supposed to do when hung from a tree.

Mabel pushed her off the chair and she began kicking her legs, her face looked so scared. We all ran in the house yelling for Dot. Dot ran outside, grabbed Pokey, and held her up. Dot was panicking and yelling for me to go get a butcher knife. I ran into the house as fast as my little legs could go, and I got the knife out of the kitchen drawer. I gave it to Dot, and she cut Pokey down.

I was seven and I knew Dot probably was not going to care that I was just a seven-year-old little girl. Mary spared punishment because she was not outside with us. After Dot finished consoling and comforting Pokey, she went outside to get some switches off the hanging tree. Lord, we knew what size switch she was going to come back with. Mabel, Dottie Mae, and I were sitting in the living room already crying. Pokey was sitting on the sofa sniffling and looking at us. When we were older, we had to go outside to the hanging tree and get our own switches. We had better not come back into the house with a small, thin switch.

Dot came back with a switch as big as a tree trunk. No one wanted that. I got it because I was the oldest; Dottie Mae got it because she should have run and told Dot what we were doing. Mabel got a couple of switches to her little legs and told to go sit down in the chair in the living room. Mabel knew how to play it up to Dot. Dot fell for it every time. Mabel would just sit there and suck her thumb with her fake tears. Mabel got less due to her illness.

That night with our routine bedtime prayers, Dot made us all ask God to forgive us for almost killing Pokey. We always had to say our bedtime prayers: *Now as I lay down to sleep, I pray to the Lord my soul to keep. If I should die before I wake, I pray to the Lord my soul to take.* In addition, we said grace before eating: *God is Great and God is good, let us thank him for our food, by his hands, we are fed, give us Lord our daily bread,*

9

Amen. I taught my children the same prayers, and I still use it today in teaching my great grands when they visit.

You would think we would get tired of Mabel choosing the backyard activities. However, she would suck her thumb and pout with that pitiful look in her eyes. On the other hand, Mary was not outside with us. Mary never wanted to go outside with us because she was afraid of dogs, including our own dog, which was mean and barked all the time. Mary was afraid of cats too. I always had a cat. I would feed stray cats and they would come to our front porch all the time. If William was not at home, I could have the cat in the house. I used to chase Mary with the cat through the house when Dot and William were not at home. That was the only way I could get her back or punish her. Mary always received extra attention from William and the rest of us did not. I was careful not to physically fight her, but it did not stop me from teasing her. She was thicker than I was. If she got a grip on me when we were fighting, I would be in trouble.

If Dot were home, Mary would yell, "Dot, Lou is chasing me with that cat."

I would yell back, "Dot, she is not telling the truth. She always lies on me. She hates me."

Dot would yell back, "Do not make me come out on that front porch. I swear that if I have to come out to that porch, I am not going to be empty-handed." We all knew what that meant!

On another visit, Mabel wanted us to play doctors. Mabel asked who wanted to be the patient. During these activities, Nee Nee and Bucky were present, but they did not want to be the patient because Mabel said we would have to get a needle so we could get better. She took some needles from dots sewing box and told Pokey that she would stick her just a tiny bit in her arm.

Well, what do you know? She agreed to it. I warned her not to, but Mabel convincingly said, "I live in the hospital; I know how to give needles I get them all the time."

When Mabel took that needle and stuck Pokey in her arm, she left out a very loud scream, like a hurt animal. I ran through the house as fast as I could; I did not want a whupping for that.

Dot yelled, "What is going on out there?" I told her Mabel took needles out of her sewing box to give Pokey a needle in her arm. Dot stopped ironing clothes and walked quickly to the backyard, took off one of her slides and snatched Mabel up and wore her legs out. Dot was yelling and telling her that she was going to come home one of these days and kill one of us kids. We were shocked that Mabel's tears did not help her escape that time. I think she was too!

One day I had what I thought was a good idea. Dot baked a cake and put vanilla icing on it. It was sitting on the kitchen table for later. I decided that we would make mud pies and cakes in the back yard. Making the mud pies was easy. Making the cake was difficult because the mud was too wet. Therefore, I went into the kitchen with Mabel and we took Dot's cake to the yard. We covered it with mud. We needed white icing, so I sent Pokey and Dottie Mae in the house to get Dot's bag of salt. They came back with the salt and Mabel and I covered the now muddy cake with the white salt. Then we took it to the kitchen and put it back on the table.

A little later Dot called us in to have lunch. When she stopped and looked at the cake, she said aloud, "Why is that cake falling?"

Dot touched it and tasted the icing. Dot looked at all of us like she was going to kill us. Mabel, Dottie Mae, and Pokey were all saying in unison, "It was Lou's idea."

I was scared, crying, before Dot went to get the switches off the tree. We all got a whupping for that incident. In case you are wondering, no, Mary was not outside with us. In addition to being scared of Rex, she was so girly. She would spend her time in the living room looking out the window, playing with her doll. Mary always did that. There were things that Mary liked, like playing jacks by herself. When our cousin Tiny, Aunt Almeda's daughter would come to stay with us, Mary would hang out with her because she was older. Aunt Almeda dropped her off from time to time for Dot to keep her. Aunt Almeda was not married and always on the go. We had constant visits from her and her kids. Tiny and Jimmy Jackson were her children.

One summer afternoon, our next-door neighbor, Joanie, came over to play with us. Dot had just washed, hot combed, and braided her hair with two braids and a bang that morning -- a style most moms used on Codorus Street for their little girls. Mary decided we would play hairdresser with Joanie. Mary had Mabel undid her hair while Dottie Mae went to get dirt in her sand bucket. When she returned, Mary told Joanie to bend over on the step while she washed her hair with the dirt.

Joanie started crying because dirt got in her eyes. She ran home next door. Her Grandma, Miss Bertha, came over to our house yelling to Dot, *your kids did this to Joanie.* Dot apologized and told her she would do Joanie's hair over. Dot looked at us, Mary, Mabel, and me, and said, "Get upstairs." Miss Bertha took Joanie home to get a bath and wash her hair. She returned with Joanie a little while later and Dot redid her hair.

After Joanie went back home with her Grandma, Dot came upstairs. She had graduated from switches to a belt. I could deal with that, as it was much smaller than Williams' truck belt with the large silver buckle. That buckle had lit into me more times than I care to recall. You could say William and I were at odds with one another on more than one occasion due to our love hate relationship.

I jumped in front, as I wanted to get it over with first. There is nothing like watching your sister getting a whipping and waiting for your turn. We always counted our belt marks to see who had the most welts. They would be red and hurting.

Chapter 3
Survival

Holidays, Christmas, Easter, Halloween, Fourth of July and our birthdays came and left, year after year, along with playing in the backyard and getting more than my share of beatings when William came for a few days. He never stayed long. Dot did not have much money, but she always made the house pretty, and the aroma of her cooking was so nice to smell during the holidays.

At Christmas time, she always baked pies, cakes and large cans of cookies. She would count them out to us so they would last. We would always check to see if someone got more than the other one. We made sure to tell Dot if they did. Dot would put lights in the windowsills, usually blue. Somehow, William always showed up on Christmas Eve, maybe two nights before, smiling and in a good mood.

One Christmas when Mabel was home for a visit from the hospital, she had gifts for all of us. Apparently, the hospital took her shopping to buy her siblings a gift. Easter was always a good time too, painting Easter eggs with Dot? Dot loved hiding Easter eggs from us. We would hunt for them and whoever found the egg that Dot drew on, which was a woman's face smoking a cigarette, would get a quarter to spend at the corner store. William missed most of those times.

Our cousins, Franny and Shirley, spent many nights at our house, as we did with them at Aunt Sis's house on Freys Avenue and later, the Parkway Projects. Aunt Sis always had cakes and cookies for snacks -- not fig bars, pretzels and peppermint patties like Dot.

Halloween was fun until Dot got the bright idea that everybody needed to have about the same amount of goodies. Dot would take everybody's goodies, dump them in large tin can, and give us five or six pieces of candy when she wanted to. She tied that candy to our behavior and schoolwork. In my little head, I was never going to do that when I got my own kids.

Summer 1955, things were very hard for Dot. William was home less and less. It became painfully evident that he stayed on the road making stops not just for his job but stops with other women. Whenever he was home, he would find a reason to pick on Dot and for every little thing. Mabel and I used to hear her praying in her room for God to take care of us.

I used to tell Mabel not to worry because when we grew up, we would take care of her and beat up William if he tried to hurt her.

It should be noted, that Dot did not know how to drive and had to depend on our neighbors for help with all of us. As if things could not get any worse, Dot delivered a baby boy Clifford Earl (Bucky) on September 25, 1955. William finally got his boy. Dot finally had permission to get her tubes tied. Dot was tired after birthing seven children who could blame her. In those days, the father had to sign a consent form for a wife to have the procedure that would prevent pregnancy.

The buggy is now too full because only five of us could ride in it at a time. Bonita, Pokey, and Bucky always had a spot because they were the babies. Mabel had a spot because of her heart condition. Dottie Mae had a spot because she was very short, and she could only take small steps. Dot was always worried because Dottie Mae was not getting any taller. She would always ask Dr. Rosenberg when he made house visits to examine us for routine care, if Dottie Mae was going to grow. He would tell her not to worry; she will catch up with the other kids. Finally, on one of the home visits Doctor Rosenberg told Dot that Dottie Mae was going to be a midget or a dwarf. Dot always knew there was some reason why Dottie Mae was not growing like the rest of us. Dot was sad but knew she could not change that. Mary and I had to walk because we were the oldest. Mary would complain the whole time we had to walk; she was chubby and got tired out quickly. She would sit on the ground and have tantrums. Dot just kept on walking and yelling to her to stay there. However, after we had taken a few steps, Mary would get up, run after us, and grab on to her side of the buggy.

September 1955, it was now time for me to start school. The school district assigned me to Lincoln Elementary while Mary was at Princess Street School. Dot tried hard to get the city to change it so Mary and I could be at the same school. The school system would not budge. Dot arranged for Sammy Carrol, one of our next door neighbors, to walk me to and from school on his way to and from his school. It was cool; he brought me candy all the time, and I did not mind the separation from Mary now. Besides, Dot said I was a big girl and had to do things without my big sister sometimes.

Our house at 480 Codorus Street was cozy when it was only Dot and us. Codorus Creek was behind our house, as it was for all families who lived on the creek side of Codorus Street. We did not want to encounter any Codorus Street rats. They showed up often, especially if it rained hard and long. The rats would run to our houses to keep from drowning. Sometimes they would be on the trap and Dot had to come and get them from wherever they were. One afternoon while Bonita and Bucky were taking a nap, Dot went upstairs to check on them and a rat was in the crib with Bucky. We heard her screaming and hollering. She soon ran down the stairs with Bucky and Bonita and told us about the rat. She told us we could not sleep in that room until she caught that rat. She put traps everywhere and told us not to go near them. She caught that big rat and burned it up in our kitchen coal stove. Dot was not scared of any old rat. She would get her shovel, scoop it up, and throw it into the coal stove.

One summer morning we were all at the breakfast table waiting for Dot to come downstairs to fix our breakfast. Dot walked into the kitchen and looked startled.

She yelled, "Nobody moves. Put your feet up in your chair."

Dot walked over to the large cooking coal stove and picked up her shovel. She removed one of the covers on the stove. She walked back to the table and scooped up a large river rat caught in the rattrap, and it was trying to get out. Dot walked quickly over to the stove and dropped the rat and the trap into the fire. Dot told us all we could put our feet down.

We all did…but Mary. Bucky said to Dot, "Dot, Mary didn't put her feet down."

Dot looked at Mary and told her it was ok to put her feet down. Mary started crying and asking Dot, "What if the rat comes back?" Dot told her it could not come back because she burned it up in the fire. Bucky was little, and he was not scared. Mary Elizabeth, scaredy cat, finally put her feet down. She was afraid of everything.

That coal stove not only used for barbequing rats. We used it to heat water for bathing and washing dishes. Dot always used cold water for washing laundry. You guessed it; Dot and William had a very large tin tub for bathing all of us.

It felt good getting a nice hot bath after a long day outside playing in the heat. The babies were first. Mary and I were always last. The water would be warm by now. It was still better than being cold. Dot added hot water until everyone had his or her bath. We all hated when William helped to bathe us, because he would scrub our knees so hard to get them clean. Dot would tell him that it was the color of our skin, not dirt. He thought he could scrub off our complexion, especially for me, Mabel and Lugenia. We were darker than the other kids were, and William's complexion was medium caramel brown.

William was not bad all the time; we actually missed him when he was gone for a long time. We would look out the window in the living room when we knew he was supposed to be coming home, jumping up and down when we saw him. Somehow, Dot always knew when he was expected. (Now I know what Maya Angelou meant when she said, "I know why the caged bird sings.") He would pull up in his big tractor-trailer truck and come in the house; we all would run to him full of excitement and enjoyed the moment for we did not know how long it would last.

Chapter 4

Growing Up with Mixed Emotions

TIME ROLLED ON IN 1957. William came and went as usual. His moods were still unpredictable. Sometimes he was in a good mood and sometimes he was not. William and Dot would sometimes have company over to our house. The company would be all of our aunts and some of our uncles and a few neighbors from across the street. Aunt Vera, Uncle Herman, Aunt Emma, and Uncle James, Uncle LeeBoy, Uncle Joe and some others. William would be on his best behavior and so very nice to everyone. He really had two personalities and wore them both with perfection: the abuser, and the good person. We children would listen while sitting on the steps and watch them dance.

Dottie Mae loved it when Dot and William had company. She played up her midget life. Everyone thought she was so cute. They did not know she was older than she appeared. Dottie Mae was good at having a stash of quarters when everyone left. Dot spanked her many times for begging for quarters.

One of their friends that stick out in my mind was Mr. Bill Duncan. I loved him; I used to tell him that William was beating up on Dot. He gave me his phone number and taught me how to call him collect the next time it happened. I did call him from time to time. I just had to dial zero on the telephone and ask the operator to make a collect call for me. She would ask me for the number, and I would tell her, along with my name. Back then, telephone numbers were only five numbers, and it was easy for me to memorize them.

This one particular time I called him to tell him about William being mad because I lost his boot in the water when he took me fishing. It was a time before Bucky and Bonita were born; we used to go fishing a lot. William, Dot, Mary, Dotti Mae, and I went fishing often. Mabel was in the hospital again this one time. I loved walking through the water until William punished me for losing his boot in the water. We fished under the old Columbia Pennsylvania Bridge. This one particular fishing trip, William put a pair of his fishing boots on me to walk through the water with him.

He was looking for a good spot on some rocks. Everything was going well until William decided to walk back over to the dry area land where Dot was sitting with my sisters to get more bait. I decided to follow him because it was scary over there without him. While I was trying to wade through the water to get to him, one of the boots came off in the water; I could not see through the water to get the boot. I started yelling for him to come and get me and when he picked me up, I only had one boot. He put me down in the water and told me to find the boot.

He stood there while I was crying frantically to feel through the water for the boot, wiping my eyes and calling Dot. Dot asked him to bring me over and he would not. He just left me standing there in the water. Dot got up, walked through the water, and found the boot. Dot was so brave to come into the water and get me out. Everything was quiet; my siblings were crying now, too, and hugging me when I got over to them. I never ever went into the water or ever wanted to when we went fishing again. I was so afraid of the water after that. I would just look for seashells to wash and paint when we got home.

Mr. Bill would always tell Dot that I called. I do not know what they talked about, but Dot told me I had to ask her whenever I wanted to call him. Maybe it just made me feel safe when talking to him. He would come back into my life later on.

When William was in a good mood, I wanted to love him, I really did. We did many things together. He used to take Mary and me to horse buggy racing at the York Fairground. Some days he would be nice and would pack all of us in his Oldsmobile for a scenic ride through the York countryside -- four people in the front and five in the back seat. There were no seatbelt laws back in those days. We would go for ice cream. I loved vanilla and strawberry. We also would go on a drive to Uncle Herman and Aunt Vera's house on Duke Street, where Mary and our cousin Charles would have eating contests. On Sundays, William would drive us to Columbia, Lancaster County Pennsylvania, to see our Nanny. Sometimes we would go to see Aunt Sis. Aunt Sis was my Dad's only sister. She taught all of us how to swear. Dot did not like us swearing. She certainly did not approve of Aunt Sis teaching us how to swear. We were good at it too. Dot would say to her, "They are girls, Sis."

One summer day summer in 1957, William came home and had a present for Mary. We all heard his big truck outside roaring down the street. We would run and jump on the couch and look out of the window for him. He got out of the truck with a two-wheeled Columbia pink and white bike with training wheels. William called Mary to come outside to see the bike. He said, "Look what I got for you." Mary was so happy; she ran outside and climbed on it, with William's help.

I said, "William, where is my bike?"

He said he would get me one the next time. I hated him that day. I truly knew then that he loved Mary and not me or my other siblings. All of my siblings were watching Mary ride her bike while William was holding the back of it so she would not fall. Not me, I ran into the house to cry to Dot. When she figured out what happened, she hugged me and said, "Lou, I will save enough money to buy you a bike," and she did. It was just as nice as Mary's but only purple and white.

I realized at that time that William did not favor me in any way. A few weeks later on one of William's return home visits, he brought me and Mary metal roller-skates with keys. We were happy because they would be better than the wooden skates we had to learn to skate with in the past. I think he was trying to make up for what he did to me with the bike episode.

I did not trust him ever again after that. I knew I had to watch my step. Contention between my sister and I was always tense after that time. All because of William, for we were both children.

It would not be long before he showed his true colors again. Sometimes his face would look very mean so we would quickly sit down and be quiet. I could read his mood on his face. This one particular evening, summer of 1957, he came home and had that look on his face. We scrambled for our seats and sat close together. Mary told us all to keep quiet.

I knew Dot was in trouble. I wanted to be a big girl now so I could help Dot. I knew I would be able to help her one day, but I wanted it to be now. I knew at five or six years of age, that there was no way in hell I chose William to be my Father. God put me in this family to look out for Dot and my siblings. I still feel that way today.

He walked right past us through the living room, to the dining room. It was a nice summer evening. We had just finished dinner. An older white couple came and knocked at our back door asking for food and Dot let them come in the kitchen to eat some of her spaghetti. They thanked her and left. She told us always help anyone who needed help if we could. Someone in the neighborhood was always helping us.

Dot asked William if he wanted to eat; he gave her a nod of yes. She walked to the kitchen to get his food. She placed his plate in front of him. William was sitting at the dining room table. He stared down at the food for a while then stood up quickly, threw his plate through Dot's china cabinet, turned it over, and upset the table.

By this time, all of us were crying. Everyone but me was crying very loudly and asking William not to hurt Dot. He turned to us and said shut the hell up. I was crying silently, yes, tears were falling from my eyes too, but anger tears. I was praying in my head for God to stop him. After all, Dot told us God sees everything we do. I wondered about that many times as a child. Maybe he does not like Dot. In my little head I vowed to one day, get him back for hurting Dot.

He started towards her, and she pushed past him, running up the stairs; he ran after her, and when she was halfway up, William grabbed her and threw her back down the stairs. Then he came down and picked up Mary's pink and white Columbia bike and threw it on top her. He started kicking her. She just lay there, absorbing blow after blow. We all thought she was dead.

He stopped kicking her and bent over her swearing at her. I was now nine years of age. Something made me try to help her. I was frantic, nervous, but I picked up a lamp and hit him over the head with it, and he fell over top of Dot.

I ran as fast as I could to a neighbor's house, Miss Carrie Williams, who had two teenage daughters, Leona and Ruth Anne. They lived next door to Aunt Ginny and Uncle Herman Hawkins. She was sitting on her porch; William was right behind me. I was screaming and crying, shouting, "William Killed Dot."

I made it to her steps before William caught me. Miss Carrie stood up, pushed me into her front door, and blocked William from grabbing me. Miss Carrie told William she would send me home later after I calmed down.

Miss Carrie Williams was not quite truthful with William when she told him that. She telephoned my grandma, Mabel Paul Smallwood (William's Mother), and told her that William was beating on Dot again. Miss Carrie walked me home after she saw a car pull up in front of our house. She told me to call her if I needed her to call my grandma. I had her five-digit telephone number memorized.

My two uncles were in that car, my Uncle James and my Uncle Joe Walter. When we went into the house, Dot was in the dining room crying and cleaning up the broken glass from her china cabinet. My siblings were with her, and they were crying too. Uncle James asked Dot where William was, and she told him upstairs. Both uncles went upstairs, and they were not smiling. We could hear Uncle James fussing William out for hitting Dot. After a while, William came downstairs grabbed his hat off the end table and left with some clothes in his hands.

That was the first time we realized William was not so tough. They made him leave the house. We were so happy and asked Uncle James and Uncle Joe if they could live with us so William would not come back. Uncle James said; we will see, and they left after talking to Dot a little while. Dot had two bruised eyes and a busted lip and bruised legs. She was holding her side, probably hurting from the kicks she took to her body and the bike thrown on top of her. I wished my two uncles had kicked William in his sides and threw a bike on him so he could have felt what Dot was feeling.

We were all so happy that William left the house. I prayed that he would never come back home. We knew he would return to get his truck soon for work. We knew we would be okay for a week or two. I apologized to Dot for breaking her lamp. She told me not to worry it was not my fault. She said she would save some more Ballantine beer bottles and make another lamp soon. She spent so much time making it out of a Ballantine beer bottle and knitted a cover over it. She was talented like that. She made lamps, curtains, and clothing for us. What she could not make she purchased from rummage sales. We loved going to the rummage sales with her. She would give us $1.00 and we could shop while she was shopping. We took turns going with her to the rummage sales.

It did not take long for William to return home. When he did, he was the same man. Nothing changed. He was nice at first and then his same old self. One afternoon while he was home, Mary and I were skating in our backyard (the concrete part of our yard, near the alleyway). Most of the row houses had alleyways. We were skating, and we needed to tighten our skates with our skate key. Mary lost her skate key and wanted to use mine. I told her she could use it when I was finished with it. I was leaning over tightening my skate when Mary knocked me over and took my skate key. I felt I had no choice but to defend myself and get my skate key back. Therefore, I got up off the ground, took my skate off, and hit her with it, probably a few times. Mary started hollering, as if I was killing her.

When William came outside, Mary was still hollering all over the place. William took off his large leather truck belt (with the large gold buckle) and gave her two hits. He gave me too many hits to count. I lay down in a ball on the concrete ground and tucked my head. I had no more cry in me to give. Dot was observing through a side window. She ran out to the backyard and tried to get William off me. He started swearing at her and pushed her away, but he did stop whupping me. I knew then that there was no way possible I chose him for my father. This incident was further confirmation for my strained relationship with William.

December 1957 – We had a special Christmas. Dot was in Christmas Holiday mode. She baked large cans of cookies and changed all the light bulbs in the house downstairs to blue, as she usually did. William would find a Christmas tree for us, and we would decorate with Dot and William. This year, Christmas Eve was so special. We stayed up later than we usually did. I remembered it snowed that evening. Around ten in the evening, there was a knock on the front door; it was Mr. and Mrs. Santa Clause, and they had toys for all of us. It was an awesome treat. William was on his best behavior, as he usually did when someone was watching. Dot told me later that William's job put the Christmas event on for our family. Our family chosen because we had a very big family compared to other families he worked with. School Christmas break was quiet.

No matter what William did to Dot and us, she never left him, and he never apologized for what he did. Dot felt trapped with seven children, no driver's license or car and no real money to support us. She would not confide in her mother because she was embarrassed to run to her. Dot was not from York, Pennsylvania and did not have family there. She had a sister in Lancaster, Pennsylvania and a brother in New York with several children of his own.

Chapter 5

Neighbors in the Codorus Street Bubble

S UMMERS WERE FUN IN THE Codorus Street Bubble. For six years
from 1952 – Jan 1958, the years moved quickly: Christmas, Easter,
spring and then summer. Mostly all of the families were connected.
The Haymon, Drayden, Saxon, Troutman, Bridgett, Roscoe, Smith,
Johnson, Maxfield, Hawkins, Kearse, Addison, Warren, Walker,
Kirkland, Thompson, Owens, Staley, Leckrone, Mobley, Hughes,
Wright, Orr, Williams, Noldens, Carrols, Berkheimer, Messersmiths,
Kinards, Rickter, Hires, Burket (she was our next door neighbor),
Padgett, Grimes, Dagins, Jennings, Nimmons, Garvin, Dowling,
Handy, Eyster, Mitchell, Buchannan, Gilberts, Charms, and us the
Smallwood's. These families comprised the Codorus Street Bubble. We
had block parties and parents had house parties; there were several other
bubbles where Negroes lived. To name a few, Frey's Avenue, South
Newberry Street, Orange Way, West Newton Avenue, to name a few.
Many of the areas were substandard housing. Parents worked together
and children played together. It was my time to make friends outside
of our house, like my siblings. Then finally, we were old enough to
walk to Sunday school alone. Just about every family went to Church

of God and Christ where Mother Walker made sure we were on our best behavior.

We played on the *real playground*, Codorus Street, the playground that we all knew best. I remember us running until we were out of breath. I loved playing marbles, especially if Arthur Hawkins was there, jumping rope, hopscotch, red light, mother may I, post office (by the way, William thought I didn't like boys), riding bikes, playing hide and seek and climbing trees in the backyard. Apples, Peaches Pumpkin Pie who is not ready holler I. Those were the days of safe streets. There was always somebody's mom sitting on their front porch watching after the neighborhood kids. Dot would give us snacks, pretzels, or fig newton cookies whenever she had any spare change. Sometimes when William was not at home, there were thunderstorms and the streetlights would go out on Codorus Street, like most streets in York, Pennsylvania. Dot would let us sit in the vestibule and watch the lightning. She would take a flashlight and walk to the store to get hard candy, pretzels, and or fig newton cookies. I hate fig newton cookies today.

During the summer, white people would come to Codorus Street and set up grandiose Gospel Tents to have revivals, open air Church. Trucks from Baltimore would come on weekends to sell fresh fruit, eggs, corn on the cob, etc. Dot would buy a watermelon if she had any extra money to spare. We loved watermelon. We were having watermelon for lunch one day and while Dot was slicing it, Bucky stuck his hand under the melon. The knife sliced down right through Bucky's finger around the bone. Dot grabbed her dishrag to stop the bleeding. She had Mary hold the rag tight on Bucky's finger until she gathered some clean rags to use to wrap up his finger. Bucky was crying so much. She took off the dishrag, soaked Bucky's finger in salt water, and made sure it was clean, and then she wrapped it securely with a clean rag and taped his finger up. She would take the dressing off every two or three days. His finger eventually healed up like new. Dot was so thrifty with everything that she did. She tried to avoid emergency room visits. We did get a slice of watermelon that afternoon.

Aunt Chessie would make root beer in a big washtub for the neighbors. Mary and I walked alone to her house. It was a half block up the street from our house. Her house was on the same side that we lived on. She would be smoking her pipe and selling her root beer. She always gave us a couple bottles free because Dot would send her empty beer bottles to her sometimes. The Ballantine beer bottles were worth a nickel if Dot returned them. I would sneak to the Lewters and beg for taffy then go to Miss Bertie's house and sit on her porch for a while. I would make my rounds to Aunt Ginny Hawkins' house across the street. Aunt Ginny made fresh potato chips. Aunt Ginny and Dot were best friends. Aunt Ginny named her daughter, Sandra, after me. We were both Sandra Lee. She made clothes for us sometimes. We could walk to Mary's Sub Bar. It was on Penn Street, at the end of Codorus Street. There was a corner store, Mr. Charlie Myers, close enough for us to walk there.

One day Dot sent Mabel and me to the store to get a few items and put it on her store bill. Mabel and I decided we would get some penny candy, so we added to her list. Lord of Mercy, when she saw that bill, she flipped her lid. Who would have thought that she would notice the quarter we spent at the store? Dorothy kept track of everything she spent. She would sit down with her pencil and paper and tally everything up when she spent anything. I think now that she influenced me tremendously. Counting her money on paper helped me to be financially stable. She never knew when William would show up to give her any money. She had to be *on target* with her budget. As far as food on the table, the neighbors who went fishing and or hunting always checked to see if Dot needed meat for her family, fish, rabbit, possum, raccoon, ground hog, or pheasant. She always accepted. She would nail the dead animal to a tree skin, gut it, and then soak in salt water overnight preparing it to cook. I always volunteered to help her.

One day Dot told Mary it was her turn to hold the groundhog's foot so she could skin and gut it. Mary cried and begged, "Please Dot, do not make me hold the groundhog's foot."

The rest of us would be laughing our butts off. Dare we be caught? Dot told her she was always the first one to want seconds when she made baked ground hog, string beans with mashed potatoes and gravy.

Our next-door neighbor, Miss Alice, a white neighbor, would make soap for her family and she would share with Dot for our family. All of the neighbors looked out for each other. Food and home necessities were usually an issue if William did not come home in a timely manner. He often did just that.

People in the 1950s loved to gossip. Back-door gossip was our Facebook, Instagram and twitter. A friend told Dorothy where to find William. One early Saturday morning, Dot decided that she would go to where William was. She needed money for groceries. It was still summer. I went for a walk with Dot to a house that was on South Newberry Street. When we arrived there, she knocked on the door and a little girl answered the door. Dot asked her if William was there and she said he was upstairs in my mom's room. I waited on the porch as Dot told me to do. Dot came out of the house took my hand and we left. Dot got the money she needed to buy the household necessities. William obviously did not make a fuss. He could not get out of that. I did not know the little girl then; I later found out who she was, as well as who her mother was, when I was older.

Dot told me that William and the woman were in bed together. They started grabbing the sheets and covering themselves up. She said when she opened the door at the top of the stairs it scared them. She said that she asked William for some money to feed her kids. He told her to get his pants off the chair next to the bed and take what she needed.

Chapter 6

William's Spiraling Behavior

IT WAS BETWEEN 1958-1959 OR SO. Things at home were great when Williams was not around and tense when he finally showed up. He had learned to keep his temper in check around us, but I knew better. We never saw him hurt her again, but we knew he was hurting her when they were in their bedroom behind closed door. If she had makeup on when she came downstairs in the morning, she was trying to hide the marks on her face.

Mabel, Dottie Mae, Pokey, and I shared the same room next to their room for a while, and we could hear her cry and say she was sorry. Mabel and I would cry and talk about how we hated William. Mabel always sided with Dottie Mae or me. This one particular night when we were about five or six years of age, we heard Dot whimpering, and a thought came to my mind. I decided to run it by Mabel. After all, we always go along with her ideas. I told her we could sneak some rat poison into William's food when Dot fed him. I told her he would die like the rats Dot caught in the traps, and we could help Dot burn him up in the coal stove.

Mabel was worried about that plan; she was worried that Dot would not get any money to feed us. I agreed with her and decided that we were not strong enough to help Dot put him in the coal stove anyways. William must have felt some kind of way when he saw us in the morning. It was as if he knew we were plotting against him. He decided that Mabel, Mary, and I would start sleeping in the attic so we could not hear what was going on in their room anymore. Dot did not want us to sleep in the attic because it was not finished, and birds and bats could get in there. Mary was so afraid up there, Mabel and I used to make noises at night to scare her. Almost every night, Mary would yell, "William, there is a ghost up here." Mabel would be yelling, "I want a glass of water" She thought she was still in the hospital where she could yell for anything she wanted whenever she wanted to. William would come upstairs or Dot and turn on the light on a pull string and give Mabel a glass of water. They would show Mary that there was no ghost in the attic. Mary would not buy that. William got tired of her yelling "a ghost is up here, help us" and moved us back downstairs. I had to sleep on the side of the room far from their bedroom door on the second floor so I could not hear what was going on in their bedroom. Mary was scared of everything -- dogs, cats, birds, worms, etc. I used to scare her with cats, dogs, and worms when Dot was not paying attention. I never scared her when William was around. That would have been a death sentence for me. He was so temperamental.

One evening, Dot was cooking and soon after, it was dinnertime. At that time, we were at the age to help ourselves get our own food to put on our plates. Dot had a rule that if you put it on your plate, you had to eat it. Children in foreign countries were starving, she would tell us. Dinner looked good, mashed potatoes, corn and fried chicken or so we thought it was mashed potatoes. William just happened to be home this evening. The whole family said grace. Mary was the first to put a big spoon of mashed potatoes in her mouth. Mary said, "These mashed potatoes are spoiled, Dot."

Dot replied they were not mashed potatoes. It was squash. We all tasted the squash, and no one liked it except Bonita and Bucky. They asked for butter and ate theirs as if they were eating mashed potatoes. Mary kept asking to go to the bathroom on the back porch because she had an upset stomach. Upset stomach my foot! I was on to her. She would fill her mouth up with the squash, go to the bathroom on the back porch, and spit it out. No way in hell, that William would have excused me from the table that many times.

Mabel, Dottie Mae, and Pokey got theirs down somehow. I just could not do it. I was last at the table and sat there for about two hours until William got mad as hell and sent me to bed. I knew this was not a good sign.

Another time, he tried to make me eat a piece of beef. I did not like meat very much when I was a little child. One day I had eaten a piece of beef or so Dot and William thought I did. I chewed it until I could not chew anymore and then just held it in my jaws. I pretended as if I could not open my mouth. Dot was scared; she thought I was having a lockjaw experience. Dot convinced William to take me to the York Hospital. They did. I would not open my mouth for the doctors and nurses. Then a nurse came in with a dish of goodies. Lollipops all colors. She said I could have some if I opened my mouth. Dot was watching me and so was William. I opened my mouth and spit the chewed-up meat out. Dot was so happy that I did not have lockjaw. William was looking at me, like *wait until I get your ass home.* William was laughing in the car on the way home. To my surprise, he asked me for one of my lollipops. I gave him one. He was so nice to Dot and me on the way home. I did not get a beating that day. The lollipops saved me.

35

The next morning when everyone was having scrambled eggs, sausage, and biscuits, William sat my hard ass white squash in front of me and said this is what you get to eat for breakfast. Dot looked over from the stove (I was thinking, Dot do not say anything) and said, "William she cannot eat that food cold."

William responded, "Then heat it the hell up because she is not getting nothing else to eat. She should have eaten it last night when it was hot. If she does not eat it now, she will have it again tonight for supper."

Everyone was done eating breakfast, and I was still at the table looking at that squash. William let me sit there for what seemed like an eternity. He walked by me and took off his big, thick truck belt with the big silver truck buckle. He was threatening me non-verbally. I was so scared. He snatched me up by the arm, I jerked away from him and said, "Leave me alone you bastard," and ran through the house up the stairs, and Mabel was right behind me. There was that trunk at the top of the stairs in the first bedroom. Mabel opened it and told me to get in. I jumped in. It took William a while to come up the steps; he knew I had nowhere to go.

I heard his footsteps coming up the steps and he was saying, "You might as well come out Sandra Lee." Mabel said he was looking under the beds in our rooms. He did not see me so he went up to the attic. He came down from the attic and asked Mabel where I went. I heard Mabel tell him that I ran out of the front door. Even Mary tried to help me, saying I was outside. It seemed like I was in that trunk forever again; I kept telling Mabel I could not breathe. She would lift the trunk for a few minutes at a time so I could get oxygen. Dot came upstairs and Mabel showed her where I was. She lifted me out of the trunk, squeezed me tightly, and said, "He is gone Sandra Lee." I was crying and telling Dot that William was going to get me when he came back. The next time he came home, he did not beat me. I guess he must have forgotten about it.

We were all getting older and Dot decided that she needed a part-time job. She found one in a local factory. She had to figure out who was going to take care of us while she was at work. She asked our paternal grandmother, Grandma Mabel Paul Smallwood on West Gas Ally if she would keep us and she agreed. We had to walk several blocks from Codorus Street to West Gas Alley (now called West Gas Ave, that house still stands today) to Grandma Mabel's house. The first thing Grandma Mabel taught us was what to do if we heard the bomb threat sirens when we were outside and happened to be close to the corner store, where we were allowed to go to buy penny candy when she had some change. The store was on the left corner of the alley. We were to go inside the store, and they would sit us in the basement bomb shelter until all was clear for us to go back to her house. I was not feeling that. I kept thinking about rats being in the basement, like at our house. If we were home with Grandma, we were to go into her basement; we never had to go to her basement. I was sure glad because I did not want to run into any rats if they were down there.

Dot only worked a few days a week and boy, we were glad. The big kids that would be Mary, Mabel, Dottie Mae, Pokey, and me when at grandma's house had to go to Farquhar Park all morning long until after lunch. It was a long walk, so we would take a short cut across the railroad tracks. We had to be sneaky because if Miss Booth saw us, we would be in big trouble. She and grandma were friends. We had to pass Miss Booth's house to get to the railroad tracks. That was a challenge. We had to walk about two blocks up a hill to cross the tracks.

When we got there, we had to climb down a steep hill to get to the tracks, cross the tracks and then climb up a steep hill to get to the park. Mary always cried and was afraid to climb down the hill; Mabel and I had to help her go up and down the hill. The park was fun for a while but then it was the same old thing: pick honey suckles, play in the sand box and on the swings, and monkey bars. One day Mary decided that she had enough of Farquhar Park. She told Dot that we had to go to the park every time we were at grandma's house from early in the morning until after lunch. Grandma required us to go to the park whenever we were at her house. None of us or the other kids from the area had a watch. Therefore, I do not know how we knew when it was time to leave the park to go back to grandma's house. Mary always told us when it was time to leave the park. Dot decided that we could stay at home by ourselves for three days a week. It went very well. Dot had extra money to shop at the rummage sales and we had extra snacks, fig bars, pretzels, or York peppermint patties. We were living large. We only had to stay at Grandma Mabel's house when Dot worked extra hours during the holidays.

Dot had been much more confident since she started working. She was making even more money doing hair. She was the local hairdresser for many of the women and little girls on our street. Her hair and makeup always looked good. This one particular evening, Aunt Sis and Aunt Vera stopped over. Looking back now, I know that they were up to no good. Dot was dressed when they arrived. They were looking in the mirror and posing. Aunt Vera had a car so she was the driver. They left the house all hyped up. My maternal grandfather, Charley Jackson, was staying with us for the weekend, so he was the babysitter that night. It was late when they came back from their girl's night out, and they were talking a mile-a-minute in the kitchen. I heard them come in. Grandpop was asleep. I planted myself on the stairs and listened secretly. They grabbed a quart of beer from the fridge and poured themselves a glass.

Aunt Sis said; "Guess he won't be driving all over town running women for a while," Aunt Vera and Dot joined in laughing. They hung a little while and then Aunt Vera and Aunt Sis left to go home. Aunt Vera had to take Aunt Sis home. The next morning when William showed up, we were all in the kitchen. He told Dot that somebody put sugar in his tank last night (Friday Night).

Dot said, "Why would somebody do that?"

William said, "I do not know, but when I find out I am going to shoot the son-of-a-bitch."

My siblings and I were all sitting at the breakfast table but only I knew what happened. I was a little scared because if William found out who put the sugar in his tank, he would shoot Dot, Aunt Vera, and Aunt Sis. When no one was around, I told Dot I knew what she did. I told her the whole story. She made me promise not to tell anyone about it, not even my siblings. I had to cross my heart and hope to die if I did. I did not want to die because I would not be able to be with my brother and sisters anymore.

The house was never the same after that situation of the sugar in William's tank. William was home more because he had no working car temporarily. He stepped up his abusive behavior with Dot. Dot came downstairs one morning to fix breakfast for us. She had face powder on trying to cover her bruised eyes. As William approached the kitchen, I looked at him with anger in my heart. If only I were big enough to stop him.

Someone had to stop him permanently.

Chapter 7

A Visit From Nanny, Margaret McGee

I TURNED TEN ON JUNE 14, 1959. It was a hot summer. William was not home much that month, just enough to be present for a few days then gone again. He brought a new Oldsmobile. He always traded his car every year. Soon after my birthday, Nanny and Mr. McGee came to our house. I thought they were coming to see us. Boy was I wrong. Nanny came to get her daughter, Dot. Nanny told Dot to gather all of her clothes and important papers she may need. She had a trunk with lots of important stuff in it. She dumped everything out of the trunk into pillowcases to take with her. Dot gathered us all into the living room with Nanny. She told us that she had to leave us for a little while, but she would come back for us soon. She made us promise not to tell William that Nanny came for her. I told Dot that it would be dark soon, and we were never away from her. We would be afraid, especially since Mary is afraid of everything, especially the dark. Dot told us we were big girls. Big girls or not, we were little kids. She said; lock all the doors when she left. There was food in the kitchen for us. She told us our Dad would be back very soon.

Dot obviously knew his schedule. I am sure now that she called his boss to find out when he was due back. She told us later that she told his boss that one of the children was sick and that she needed him to come home.

William came when it was almost dark outside. We were somewhat glad because we did not want to be in the house alone. William asked where Dot was. We all said in unison, *we do not know.* He picked up the phone and called Aunt Sis to see if she had seen Dot. Aunt Sis told him she had not seen Dot. He went upstairs and saw that Dot took all of her clothing and emptied the truck of valuable papers. He was furious. Now he knew Dot had left him.

For a few days, he was trying to care for us. He was platting our hair. We had single big plats all over our heads. He was doing laundry at the laundry mat around the corner, and washing our clothing together, and fixing our food. About three days out, he brought a young woman; I will call Sarah, to our house to watch us while he was going to be out on the truck. He told us we had to respect her because she was doing him a favor caring for us. The next day William went out on the truck. The woman slept in Dot's room until William returned home. When Sarah came downstairs, she cooked breakfast for us. She called us in the kitchen to eat.

Mabel looked at her and said, "Bitch we are not eating that food."

Mary said, "We only eat Dot's food."

Mary went and got plates out of the wooden cabinet for us and gave us peanut butter and jelly sandwiches for breakfast. Later on that evening, we were hungry again and Mary gave us cereal for supper with sugar water. We had no milk.

The next day Mary was running out of ideas. We had a coal stove and did not know how to make a fire. Therefore, we had cereal again

41

and bread with butter and sugar. The third day William came home Sarah told him what we did. He was so mad, but he did not beat any of us. He went out for a little while and got our cousin, Dolores, to take care of us. We knew her and she knew how to cook and keep the coal stove fire going. We were missing Dot and I started to think she was not coming back for us.

A few weeks went by. We could not play outside on Codorus Street, but Dolores did let us go to Bantz Park not too many blocks from home. That turned out to be an ordeal. One of the best things at the park was a community pool. We were not to take our sneakers off because kids were stealing sneakers if you left them out and went into the pool. Well Dottie Mae and Pokey decided they would get into the pool. When they got out, they had no tennis shoes. When we arrived back home, Dolores saw that they had no sneakers and decided she would punish them. She took off her flip-flop and wore them out. From that day on, we did not like her, but we did listen to her because we knew what she was capable of doing.

One afternoon, Dot showed up with Mr. McGee, her stepdad, who raised her and her siblings. We were so happy to see her. Dot knew Dolores was there, as she had been talking to her all the while on the telephone when she was gone. Delores told her William's schedule.

Dot had big burlap bags, and she took some pillowcases from the upstairs linen closet. She had us go to our rooms and empty all the drawers of our clothing. In addition to clothing, we could bring all of Dot's records, record player, and spindle. We each also took one toy, and we had to fit into Mr. McGee's car. There were five of us in the back seat and three of us in the front seat with Mr. McGee. Dolores told Dot she could walk home.

We left Codorus Street for good. I knew I would miss my friends. I was so saddened to leave them, especially Arthur Hawkins and Major Gilbert. Our mothers thought Arthur and I would grow up and get married one day.

I ran into Arthur at his father's funeral when we were adults and he said to me, "Dot had to be so slick taking you from York." We laughed because my mother was indeed a very smart woman.

As the car drove away from Codorus Street where all the kids were playing outside, a tear rolled down my face. I thought, *Good-bye Codorus Street.* I always played marbles with Arthur Hawkins, Major Gilbert, and Jesse Padget in front of Major's house. I thought we would always live at 480 Codorus Street. My siblings were also sad about leaving.

Chapter 8

Hello 554 Avenue H

JUNE 1959, WE ARRIVED AT our grandma Margaret (Nanny) and
Mr. McGee's house in Columbia, Lancaster County Pennsylvania.
My uncle Charles and Mr. McGee came outside to help us to get our
belongings out of the car and into the house. We found out early on
that living at nanny's house was not like when we came to visit for a
day or so. There were serious rules. No swearing; that was going to
kill us. If Nanny caught us swearing, it was a whipping and our mouth
washed out with soap. We did not want whippings. That did not scare
me too much because I was used to getting whippings by William's
trucker belt, which he used on me too many times to count. My siblings
would have a harder time because they did not get the large leather belt
whippings as I did.

Well, we did fairly well without swearing. Dottie Mae was caught
once or twice. She learned quickly to watch her mouth. Mabel could
swear more than any one of us. She was not planning on any whippings
from Nanny, who was a short heavy woman. After witnessing our
sister Dottie Mae getting a whipping from Nanny, we did not want to
experience it. Nanny's house was nice, warm, and safe from William.
It had a very large concrete front porch like the one on Codorus Street,

living room with a television, dining room, and kitchen on the first level. Upstairs were three bedrooms and a bathroom. There was also an attic with two rooms. That is where we all slept, all eight of us. We could play outside in the alley and walk to the store alone until William started coming to Nanny's house, looking to steal us from Dot.

One day he showed up outside and we saw him and ran for Nanny's front door, yelling for Nanny. Nanny was sitting in the living room watching television. She came out quickly. He parked his car in front of the house. He came up to the front steps and demanded to see his wife. He started to walk up on the porch (three steps and a platform to the door). Nanny told him to get off her steps.

William said, "I want to talk to my wife."

Nanny said, "You do not have a wife here. I have a daughter named Dorothy Mae and you no longer control her or her children."

All seven of us and mom were peering through the windows, as well as our Aunt Joann, Aunt Carol and Uncle Charles, thinking he is going to hit Nanny. Mind you, Nanny had a bat in her hand.

Nanny said, "William, I am going to count to three and if you are not off my steps by the time I count to three, I am going to beat you like you have beaten my daughter in the past. As God is my witness, I will not tolerate you or any other man hurting my daughters. I will go to jail before I let you hurt Dorothy again."

Nanny started to count; when she got to three, William was on the concrete patio. Nanny reached back and swung that bat. William tripped backwards off the steps, barely breaking his fall, ran, and jumped into his car.

I am like, "Damn; Nanny is a bad ass. We have protection from William now."

Mabel said, "William is scared of Uncle James, Uncle Joe, and Nanny." I found out later that my Nanny was in a domestic violence relationship with my paternal grandfather, Charles Jackson (Grand Pop) when she was a young wife of his and mother at age fourteen. Apparently (per my Aunt Joanne McGee), Grand Pop came home drunk one night. Grand Pop wanted something to eat. Nanny fixed him something to eat. While she was cooking for him, he fell asleep in the kitchen chair. When she finished fixing him something to eat, she placed the food on the table in front of him. When he finally woke and found that the food was now cold, he wanted her to heat it up, and she refused. He got up from the table, she ran, and he chased her to the kitchen back door. Grand Pop put her head through the plate glass window in that kitchen door, backwards. Somehow, she managed to reach her hand behind her into a drawer next to the door, grab a butcher knife, and stab him in his right leg and pulling the knife up through his femoral artery. The kitchen was a bloody mess. She crippled him for life. Nanny's screams brought many neighbors to her door and the police followed. Grand Pop Charlie Jackson when asked did not want to press charges on Nanny. He knew she could most likely win that battle in court, for she was defending herself.

Grand Pop Charlie Jackson later reported her for child neglect because she had no means of taking care of her children. Nanny had no job, no high school education, and no skills of any kind, except being a mother. The court gave the children to Grand Pop. He, in turn, placed the children in the Pennsylvania foster care system. Nanny did not get custody of her children until five years later when she had a job and could prove she could support them.

It is now more understandable as to why Dot stayed with William for so many years and was so afraid of him. She and her sister and brother watched their mother being beat by their father on a routine basis when they were very young children.

It is July 1959 now. We were walking from the corner store and Mabel spotted William in his car. She yelled, "Run, its William!" We all ran, but Mary was too slow, and Dottie Mae's legs could not go fast enough. William got Mary first; she was screaming for us, but we could not go back for her. He got Dottie Mae next. She was crying and yelling for me.

We arrived at Nanny's' house and told her what happened. Dot was not there. She was in Lancaster applying for welfare and looking for housing for us. A few days later, Mr. McGee drove Dot to York to look for Mary and Dottie Mae. With the help of Aunt Sis and Aunt Vera, she found them. This went on several times.

The last time he found us in the local park. We were with Aunt Joann, but that did not faze William. She protected Dottie Mae this time. He only got Mary. Dot went to York again on a bus to look for Mary. She knew where to look. Surprised by William, he beat her in the streets and some strange man on South New Berry Street stopped him and got her to safety. Mr. McGee and Nanny went to get Dot from York. Dot was so hurt; she wanted to get Mary back. Nanny told Dot to let it go for now, before that man kills you. Dot agreed at that time. Nanny told her Mary was with William, and that they would figure out to get her back from him.

It became routine living at Nanny's house. Nanny used to walk downtown to pay her light bill. My siblings and I took turns walking with her. She would always stop for candy (she said it was a secret), chocolate covered cherries (I hate them today) and tell me I was her favorite grandchild. I found out later that she told all of us that and every one of us got the chocolate covered cherries or peppermint patties. She would sit in her easy chair and read the newspaper most evenings. One evening she went to her chair and sat down. No sooner than she sat down, she realized she had sat on Dottie Mae. Nanny took a minute to get up off the chair. She was a little heavy. Dottie Mae's color was gone. Dottie Mae was already white-skinned. Nanny was shaking her like a little rag doll and rubbing her to get her skin pink again. Right in front of our eyes, Dottie Mae became the favorite grandchild. Dottie Mae started sitting on Nanny's lap, while she read the newspaper every evening. She was going to milk that for all she could.

Columbia is a very small county of Lancaster, Pennsylvania; we only saw white people when we started school or walked downtown with Nanny. Aunt Joanne was five years older than I was. She taught us all the latest dances and then took Mabel, Mary and me to the local Black legion to the kiddie dances on Front Street. Dot taught us how to hand dance, slow and fast dance.

Chapter 9

The Door Was Locked, But He Still Got In!

ONE WEEKEND AUNT ALMEDA CAME for a visit with Tiny and Jimmy. She left her son, Jimmy, with Nanny when she left. We had to all take naps after lunch in the attic where we all slept in our two rooms with Dot. There was a slide lock on the inside of the door. Dot told us to use it when she was not there. One particular afternoon we were taking our mandatory nap, Jimmy crept up to the attic to our room and opened the lock some kind of way. (He is dead now and no, and I did not kill him.) I was not asleep, and Mary was not with us at the time; she was still with William. He tiptoed (I was watching him from under my blanket) over to Dottie Mae and Pokey's bed, and I sat up and told him to leave them alone. He said, "Make me."

He came over to me, pulled the covers off me. He started touching me places where he had no business, and I knew this was wrong. I hollered for Nanny. He put his hand over my mouth. He said Nanny would not believe me because she did not like my mom and her kids. I bit him and started yelling again.

Nanny yelled up to the attic and asked what is going on up there? I told her I was dreaming because I did not want Dot, my brother, sisters, and me to have to leave Nanny and Mr. McGee's house because we had nowhere to go. I held that story until my aunt died in 1991. I could have told that story to my Dot earlier but they were ride or die sisters, and I did not want them to sever their sisterhood over the situation. They loved each other.

Aunt Almeda came for Jimmy about a week later. Boy was I glad. My impossibility was God's possibility. God knew that boy had to go away from us as soon as possible.

September was approaching (we had been at Nanny's for about 3 months), and it was time for us to go to school. It was going to be different without Mary being there with us. Bonita was in kindergarten. Bucky was not in school yet. We attended Park Elementary School for about one year and then moved to Lancaster, Pennsylvania.

When Dot came home one evening, she was in a car with a man. She was never gone more than a day or two in Lancaster trying to set up things for us. *Who was that man?* It was not William. Dot introduced him to Nanny and us. His name was Nathanial. Dot apparently met him through Aunt Almeda. Dot had good news. She found a little house for us and found a job as a cook at Sturgis Hotel and Bar in Lancaster on Duke Street. We were so happy to be able to have our own house with Dot. Packing up was easy; we only had clothing, records, a record player, and important papers that Dot took from the trunk on Codorus Street.

Chapter 10

A Home of Our Own

WE FINALLY MOVED FROM NANNY'S house to Mercer Avenue in Lancaster, Pennsylvania. We were somewhat happy because now we could cuss. We were also sad because we loved Nanny. We had a small, two-story wood framed house with no attic. It had two bedrooms upstairs. There was a door with a lock on it leading to the upstairs, a dining room, living room, and kitchen on the first floor. There was no bedroom for Dot. Her bedroom was the living room with a sofa bed. We were all in school except Bucky, at Washington Elementary. Dot was a friendly person; she made friends quickly on the avenue. We all made friends at school. Dot made sure to find a Sunday school that we could attend.

Soon we started riding the Mennonite Church bus to Sunday school every Sunday. We had not been to church since we left York. Christmas came upon us fast. It was bedtime for all of us one night. I was upstairs in bed, but still awake. I could hear Dot crying, so I went to see why she was crying. *Was William down there?* I saw her sitting at the dining room table; it seemed she was at her lowest point.

I said, "Dot, what is wrong?"

She looked up at me and said, "I do not have any money to buy Christmas gifts for all of you. I found a doll for Bonita and a truck for Bucky at the rummage sale yesterday. I can make new clothes for the doll and get her hair all cleaned up, and I can paint the truck for Bucky."

I started rubbing her back and told her that Mabel and I did not believe in Santa Clause and that I would explain to Dottie Mae and Pokey that there is no Santa Clause, and if they want to be big girls like Mabel and me, they have to forget about Santa Clause.

I went upstairs to wake up Dottie Mae and Pokey. I took them to my bed, explained about Santa Clause, and told them that they cannot tell Bucky and Bonita that there was no Santa Clause for real. At first Pokey was not buying it. Dottie Mae talked her into believing me.

That Christmas it was about seventy-degrees outside, and everyone was out with shorts on. I went to visit some of my friends' houses, Barbara Jean, Gaye, and Sandra Brown. I noticed that all of my friends called their parents Mom and Dad. So that Christmas evening I had a meeting with all of my siblings, and I told them, we had to start calling Dot, Mom. We can keep calling our Dad William because he did not live with us. They agreed.

About five months into the school year (February,) William showed up to give Mary back to mom. Mary seemed so grown up. She was twelve and half years old. She knew how to smoke and drink alcohol. She tried to teach me to smoke several times. I almost choked to death and decided I did not want to smoke. She continued to smoke after school and made me promise not to tell mom.

Mary was always staying out past her curfew and always threatening to run away. Wherever she was staying in York, she obviously had no curfew. Mom had rules. Mom enrolled her in Edward Hand Junior High School. Mary made friends fast. She found out that our cousin, Joanie Stewart, was going to that same school. We had many cousins in Lancaster. Lancaster used to be one of mom's old stomping grounds when she was a teen and Aunt Almeda lived there for years. They had a younger brother named Clifford Earl, who lived in New York City. Bucky shared his name.

One day Mary and one of our cousins decided they were going to run away. I overheard them talking about it, and I told Mom about it. Mom was standing at the stove stirring a pot of stew. She did not even look up at me and said, "Let her go ahead."

I said, "Mom it's winter outside, what if something happens to her?"

Mom said, "I can't worry about that right now. Mary will come back when she is hungry and has no shoes on her feet."

She sure did return home a week or so later with no coat, no shoes and hungry, looking like she was a poor throwaway child. If that was not enough, Mary fell in love with this Italian and Black mixed boy. He was so cute, but he was in a so-called gang and lived on the other side of town where we were not supposed to travel. Our side of town, though, had its own gang, a group of boys who called themselves a gang. Mary would set me, Mabel and Dottie Mae up to fight girls she did not like because she was too old to fight them. The girl fights took place in front of gang members and anyone else on the street at that time. The girls were not a part of the gangs. Just girls Mary did not like.

This one day she wanted Dottie Mae to fight a girl that was ten times taller than she was. I told her she could not beat that girl. Therefore, she told me to do it. I said, "She is bigger than I am too, are you crazy?"

Mary said, "I am going to jump in when I see her getting the best of you." I should not have agreed to that. That girl damn near beat me to death until finally Mary jumped in and got the best of her. I should have known Mary was going to take her time. She was showing off in front of her boyfriend and his crew.

(1961) summer was approaching. It felt strange calling Dot, mom. She seemed to be okay with it. We got through the school year without any issues. By then, we knew quite a few kids. I had many friends. Mom let us join a drill team for the Elks Lodge. They loved Dottie Mae and made her the drum majorette. She replaced the girl named Debbie Warren. That did not sit well with some of the other members and the other girl's mom. Eventually they accepted her. They had no choice. We would travel to many cities to march in competition. We went as far as Chicago. The lodge did not have enough funding to take us there, so all of the members had to go door-to-door and ask for donations until we collected enough money to go. We went to the recreation center on a routine basis. Bucky, Bonita, And Pokey were too young to go. We had a specific time to be back.

This one evening, we decided to stay a little later. Mom showed up to the center looking for us. She asked the desk clerk to go and get us for her. Our friends were watching her. We were embarrassed, thinking she was going to pull that extension cord out of her purse and beat us in the street, especially since we saw her extension cord hanging out of her pocket book. Mary, Mabel, Dottie Mae, and I were walking with her home and all she kept saying was, "As soon as we get home, I am going to wear your butts out." We were quiet all the way home, about thirteen blocks. On our arrival, she told us to go upstairs and get our pajamas on. She told us she would be up there in a few minutes. We knew what was coming. We waited and waited, and she never came upstairs. I guess she was too tired to beat our butts that evening. The next morning mom told us we could not go to the recreation center for two weeks. We could only go to the local playground to play volleyball or foursquare. If we did not like it, we could sit on the front porch. Mom capped it off my saying, "Do not think I am going to forget I owe you one." I was thinking that she got a little bold since we call her mom now.

Almost time to start school again. Sixth grade, I thought I was so grown up. January 1962 was a bad year for snow; half of the time school closed because we had six to ten feet of snow. There was no weather channel to check. Mom just knew when there was no school. We could not go downstairs until mom let us out because of the lock on our door *from the outside*. Mom slept on the couch since we moved in. That was her way of having some privacy. The houses on Mercer Avenue were very close together. We lived in a fabricated bubble dictated by the government. Most Negroes lived on avenues, alleys, lanes, and crowded streets in the poor neighborhoods.

This one particular morning, it snowed so deep. Mabel decided she would open a window and talk with her friend Little Head next door. Little Head's mom was not home. She invited us over for biscuits and King Syrup. Her mom had just baked a batch of fresh biscuits the previous night. Mabel and I decided we would climb out of our bedroom window, cross the kitchen roof and go over to her house for the biscuits and King syrup. Mary wanted to come with us, then Bonita, Bucky, Dottie Mae, and Pokey wanted to come or they would tell. It was very slippery and ice and snow was on the roof. Mabel and I decided we would get the little ones down first off the roof because they were not that heavy. It was time to help Mary. Mary was scared to jump, so Mabel and I helped her to come out of the window to the roof. We both held on to her so she would not slip and fall off the roof. Since Mabel was bigger than I was, I jumped down to the ground and got Dottie Mae and Pokey to help hold Mary when Mabel lifted her down off the roof because Mary was too heavy for me alone.

We were there for a while and thought it was time to go back home. I gave Mabel a hand getting up on the roof. I lifted Bucky and Bonita up to her and she made them stand behind her. Then I had Pokey and Dottie help me to lift Mary up to Mabel so she could pull her up on the roof. Then I lifted Pokey and Dottie Mae up to Mabel. I climbed up there with little effort. When we tried to open the window, it would not open. I noticed that Mom put a nail in the window so it would not open. Everyone else was wondering what was taking me so long to open the window. I looked over at them and told them that mom nailed the window closed. Mabel and I helped everybody back down to the ground. Then we got ourselves down safely. Bonita and Bucky knocked on the kitchen door because they were so cold. Mom opened the door with the extension cord in her hand.

She said, "Just get your asses in here right now." Dot was letting the mom control go to her head just a little too much. The door we came in was the kitchen door. In ten steps or so, we were at the door in the dining room that led upstairs to our bedrooms. Bucky and Bonita got a pass because they were too young to be responsible; therefore, mom sent them upstairs and closed the door behind them. When we walked out of the kitchen to the dining room, Mary whispered to Mabel and me, "I am going last so mom will be tired."

I am the Tomboy in the family so I said, "Mom I will go first."

Mom was swinging the extension cord, and I was running around in a circle, yelling, hollering, "Yeah mom, yeah mom, I will not do it again!"

Mabel was next; her heart did not save her that time, and Pokey was next; she was already hollering while we were getting our whippings. Dottie Mae was next. When she came upstairs, her little white legs were all red with so many welts. Mabel was hugging her and rubbing her little legs.

Mary was last and she told us that mom took her flip-flops off before she got hers. We heard mom from upstairs saying to Mary, "Oh you thought I was going to be tired."

We felt sorry for Mary; it seemed like her whipping never would end. When Mary finally came upstairs, she and Dottie Mae counted to see who had the most welts. *Lord Have Mercy* that was the last time we climbed out of a window for anything. Mom had to repay Little Head's mom with a large bag of flower and a large can of King Syrup. When Mom told Little Head's Mom what happened, she got a whipping too.

Mary had a friend named Sandra Kraft, a redheaded white girl who lived about two blocks from us around the corner. Her parents owned a corner store. She would give Mary all kinds of snacks. One day Mabel and I went to the store with Mary and her friend gave us some snacks. Her dad came out of the back of the store, saw us with candy, and accused us of stealing. He said, "You niggers stay the hell out of my store. The next time you niggers come into my store, I am going to call the cops on you."

We ran out of that store so fast and went home. When we arrived home, our Aunt Almeda was there visiting mom. We told them what happened. Aunt Almeda told us to take her to that store, and we did. We walked into the store behind her. She walked up to the counter and asked to speak to the manager. The white man who chased us out of the store was standing there. He told Aunt Almeda he was the store manager and owner. Aunt Almeda reached over the counter, snatched him over the counter, and started punching him. She told him he had better not ever call my nieces niggers again. It was a big ruckus.

By now, the cops are on the scene. They handcuffed Aunt Almeda and put her in the police car. The two cops went into the store and soon came out. They let Aunt Almeda go and told her to stay away from that store. Mary and Sandra Kraft were still friends after that incident. We kept going back to that store and the owner never kicked us out of the store or called us any names again. I guess he was scared of Aunt Almeda returning to visit him again.

Nineteen Hundred and Sixty Two, the year went fast, winter, spring, summer, and fall. It was a very hot summer, and we were all outside in front of the house. Mom was playing her record player. The mail carrier just walked up to give mom her mail. Mr. Postman from the Marvelettes was playing. The song lyrics said, "Wait Mr. Postman," and the mail carrier turned around because he thought mom was calling him. He sat on the porch and she played it for him again. A few weeks later mom told us we were moving back to York, Pennsylvania. I guess mom just became homesick for York or sick of us getting into fights. She was tired of Lancaster and I guess missing Aunt Sis and Aunt Vera and her friends she left behind. We were happy, jumping up and down. We could go back to where all of our cousins lived. I was hoping we would go back to Codorus Street where all of our friends were.

We later found out that Codorus Street did not exist any longer. I found out just before we left to move back to York that my sister, Mary, was pregnant by her boyfriend, Bernard Galloway who lived in Lancaster. That may have been another reason for my mom wanting to leave Lancaster. She was going to need support and she knew the system in York better than she did in Lancaster.

Chapter 11

Time to Move Again

WE MOVED BACK TO YORK Pennsylvania in 1962. I guess mom's boyfriend, Nathanial, was taking her back and forth to York looking for a house for us. He was cool, and we saw him at our house often. He would come to take me rabbit hunting with him sometimes. I loved going hunting. He taught me how to use guns. He told me not to tell mom. It was our secret. Nathaniel never stayed over at our house and never ate dinner at our house with us. Mom did go to his house from time to time. She was always came back home at a decent time. Mom had that thing about a man staying overnight.

We moved before the school year started to a small house on Charles Lane. There was no bedroom for mom again. Mom found a job in a factory during the day and worked weekends as a cook in a local bar. The devil (William) found out we were back in York, and he started stopping by to see us. Mom was uncomfortable but stood her ground when it came to William. I was in Hannah Penn Junior High now. We were the new kids on the block. We had been gone for three years. I started noticing boys and they were noticing me. I started liking a boy named Billy Rice. There was another boy paying attention to me too, Joe Kearse (One of the Kearse kids from Codorus Street, who would have thought?) When my mom found out about him, she told me to stay away from him. He was older than I was. I think that is why mom did not want me around him. Joe started following me from school. (He did not even go to Hanna Penn). My brother, Bucky, would spy on me for mom. He would tell her every time that Joe was in front of our house when I came home from school. Every day when he would be spying on me for mom, I would see him on his skates with a soda. One day I asked him where he was getting the sodas from after school. He took me to our alleyway (a narrow passageway between our house and the neighbor's house) and pulled a soda out of the drainpipe.

I asked, "Bucky, where did you get the sodas?"

He told me he and his friend took them off the soda truck when it was parked in front of our house. Mind you, Bucky was only in second grade. I told him that they were stealing and he and his friend was going to be in big trouble if they kept taking the sodas from the soda truck.

He was quiet and started to cry. I told him I would not tell mom, if he did not tell her that Joseph was here on the porch with me after school. However, you cannot take any more soda from the soda truck when parked outside making deliveries. I told him he could go to jail.

He sniffled a little bit. I wiped his eyes and kissed him. He was good after that.

We were there for about nine months and then moved to Church Avenue, right next door to Aunt Jackie Preston (she was really our cousin). We loved Aunt Jackie. Not too many people bothered Aunt Jackie. We acclimated ourselves to the area quickly. I still attended Hannah Penn Junior High. We were happy there with mom, Aunt Jackie and our cousins, Peewee and Bobby Preston and their siblings.

Mabel and I constantly heard from mom that PeeWee was our cousin. You do the math.

Summer came quickly and two years passed; I am now 15 years of age. Mary is gone again and now has two children who live with mom, me, and my other siblings. Mary moved back to Lancaster with her boyfriend. That made me in charge again when mom was not at home. I had fun being in charge. I used to put my siblings on punishment when they showed off. I would make them stand on one leg until they were tired. Bonita and Bucky used to cry and beg to sit down for a rest, and I would let them. Mabel, Dottie Mae, and Pokey would try that, but I would just let them switch the leg they were standing on. If you could just imagine all the things, we did to get on mom's nerves.

One Saturday morning, early, Dottie Mae and Pokey thought they would see who could stick their head through the metal bedpost bars on the headboard on their bed. Apparently, Pokey went first and pulled her head out with no problem. Dottie Mae squeezed her head through the metal bars but could not get her head back through the bars. Mabel came to my room next door for help. I went to their room, and we tried to get her head back through the metal rails. I put some Vaseline on the sides of her face thinking we could get her out. Well, we could not. By now, all of us were in a panic mode, Pokey, Bonita, and Bucky crying. Mabel just standing there and sucking her thumb as if she was in shock.

I sent Mabel for mom. Mom ran up the stairs and assessed the situation. Mom went back downstairs and came back with a hammer. Mom also had a belt and whipped Dottie Mae's butt while her head was stuck between the rails. She was hollering so loud, kicking her little midget legs on the bed. When mom was through whipping her butt, she took the front part of the hammer and bent the bars open to release Dottie Mae's head. I felt sorry for her. She had welts all over her little legs. Dottie Mae told mom that Pokey was putting her head through the rails too. Well, mom went after her and whipped her butt just as she did to Dottie Mae because she said they had no business doing that.

Mary was home again from wherever she was living trying to be in charge of all of us. I would not listen to her, ever. One evening while mom was at the local bar cooking, we had a territorial fight. We had many when Mary was home. Mary would not leave out of the kitchen. She controlled the fridge. I had the living room with the television, so she could not look at television. Everyone was on Mary's side so they could eat. Mabel and I were always together in the living room. Mabel came up with an idea to trick Mary. Mabel told me she was going to tell Mary that she wanted to be on her side. She did that so she could get access to the kitchen. Mary let her be on her side. While Mabel was in the kitchen eating, she stole some food for me. When she finished eating, she left the kitchen and told Mary she was going to be on my side now. When Mary saw me eating them biscuits, she was mad as hell, called Mabel a traitor, and told her it would be a sunny day in hell when she got any more food that evening. We did not care, for we knew mom would be home soon and we could tell on her.

Mom arrived about ten o'clock in the evening, and we told on her. Mom told her off for not letting me have any food. Luckily, mom was tired. She did not get a whipping.

That night when we all went to bed, Mary had taken some food from the kitchen. I heard her over there smacking on the food. I could not wait to call for mom, who came promptly upstairs. Mary got her butt whipped because mom told us about having food where we slept. Mom did not want a rat or mouse issue.

The next night, Mary took a small knife to bed. We shared a room when she was home. Mary told me she was going to cut my throat when I went to sleep for telling on her. I was so scared.

I called downstairs to mom and said, "Mom, Mary has a knife and she said she is going to cut my throat and kill me when I go to sleep tonight."

Mom yelled back up the stairs and said to me, "Tell her that if I find you dead in the morning with your throat cut, I am going to cut her throat and kill her. Good night ladies."

I yelled with fear in my voice, "MOM!"

She said, "Go to sleep Sandra Lee, I am too tired for this mess."

"Mom; she is going to kill me."

Mom yelled back, "That is okay because I am going to kill her and even up the score for you."

I did not sleep a wink that night, while I watched Mary sleep like a baby.

Chapter 12

Card Games, Liquor, and Music

THERE WERE CARD GAMES AT Aunt Jackie's house. I collected the house cut, twenty-five cents a game, while Aunt Jackie was cooking. The house would be full, people playing cards, drinking, playing music and singing. Jim Boy, uncle Lee Boy Smallwood, Bo Gator, cousin Dicky Hawkins, Ronnie Leonard a guy who used to hang around our house with others singing and playing cards. Joe would listen to them and one day started singing with them. They were shocked that he could sing so well. He used to play music with two tablespoons while Jim Boy was playing his guitar. Soon I chimed in with them and Joseph, harmonizing and sounding good. Our house was a fun house during those times. Since Mary used to live in York with William, she had knowledge of the places to go.

Mary knew all of the spots to hang out. Freddie's on Newberry Street, Top hat, Pool Hall, all the places *we were not* supposed to be. Mary obviously stayed on Newberry Street with one of William's woman friends before. She knew her way around fairly well. One evening Mary, our first cousin Charles Smallwood and I were in Freddie's playing the jukebox when Uncle Herman (Charles' Dad) walked in through the front door. Mary and Charles saw him come in the door first and they scatted for the back door (they were standing). I was not quick enough to run with them. I saw Uncle Herman and quickly sat down next to the jukebox with my head bent down. Uncle Herman walked back by the jukebox, looked around, and left after he bought something at the counter. There was no one else in the back room where the jukebox was. I was so scared he might see me. Uncle Herman left the store; I went to the back door and told them it was safe to come back in.

Mary took me too many places where mom would not have wanted us to be. I especially loved it when Mary took me to the 615 Club on East Market Street with her and my first cousin, Shirley Miller. The years of 1963 – 1966 were years of exploring and seeing what all we could get away with. We thought we were so grown up. None of us was twenty-one years of age yet.

One night, Mary, Shirley, and I went to the 615 club out east end and I met some boy from Harrisburg, Pennsylvania. On arrival to the club at the door, the door attendant asked for identification from us. Mary said, "Do not try it; we have been coming here for a while. I can easily make a phone call to the state board; how would you like that?"

The person at the door said to Mary, "I am just trying to do my job Mary."

Shirley paid our fee to get in the club. Mary was dancing, drinking, and flirting, as was Shirley. They were sitting at a table across from me. They were smoking cigarettes, ordering drinks, and pulling out real cash. Mary had a temporary job with Manpower Services, a staffing company that hired workers for temporary work. I did not know where my cousin Shirley was working. This guy was trying to sweet talk me. The DJ was playing a record by Marvin Gaye, "Let's

Get It On." He was trying to get me to leave the club with him. The music was playing those sexy lyrics, "I've been really trying baby, trying to hold back this feeling for so long. And if you feel like I feel baby, then come on."

You know Mary and Shirley were spying on me. Just when the song got to "Let's Get It On," Mary put her cigarette out and walked over to our table. She told me she was ready to go. He had me mesmerized. When the record started talking about "giving yourself to me can never be wrong." I knew Shirley was not ready because she was talking to some cute light-skinned man with a slick wavy hair process. I think his name was Louis Johnstone or something close to that. He was looking so good. We prepared to leave. It was a long walk to East College Avenue, so we called a taxicab. That was the last time I went to the 615 Club with Mary and our cousin, Shirley Miler. I should have told on them because they were not old enough to be in the club anyways, but I did not. I may have wanted to be with them again sometime in the future.

The next day I asked Mary about her job and she told me how to apply. The following Monday, Mabel and I went to social security office on George Street to apply for a social security card. We received our social security numbers and walked to the staffing company to apply for a job. We were filling out our paperwork right next to each other when Mabel Lee was stuck.

Mabel Lee asked me in what year was she born in. I said, "I am one year older than you are Mabel."

She said, "In what year I was born?" I said to my sister, "Mabel I was born in 1949, if I am one year older than you are, in what year were you born in?"

Mabel looks at me and said, "Lou you are always trying to make things hard, everybody cannot be as smart as you are!"

I said to her, "Just write 1950. You were born in that year."

Later that day, we went to apply for the job. I sat right next to Mabel because we had to lie about our ages, and I did not want her to write 1950. She would have been very confused. Mabel was too young to apply, so I started that week with Mary who was already working.

The ride to Fort Meade seemed like such a long way from York. There were about eight of us day laborers in that van. When we arrived, we went into a large brick building, which was the dining hall. We had planned to work as long as they needed us. We worked for about a month and they no longer needed people. I heard they were hiring at a local candy factory; Mabel and I went to apply for part-time jobs for the rest of the summer, and we were hired. They accepted our fake documentation papers. They needed workers.

Mabel and I could not wait to be paid. We received our checks and we thought we were rich making $1.25 cents per hour, about thirty dollars a week. We could not wait to get home to cash checks on payday. Mom took us to the local bank, and we cashed our checks. We came outside of the bank talking about what we were going to do with our money when mom chimed in and said, "You girls have to pay rent." I forgot that Mary and I had to help with the electric bill. Mom said, "You both will be giving me ten dollars each." The both of us looked at each other as if mom had lost her mind. Mom said, "Ten dollars for rent and utilities, that is cheap."

Mabel asked mom what utilities were. I answered her and said, "The light bill."

I was so mad at mom. That was almost a third of our earnings. Mom said we ate more than that and if we wanted to go and rent a room from someone else, we could. She told us to go and try it. She knew we could not with ten dollars a week and our jobs were temporary positions.

The next day we skipped work because I convinced Mabel that we should go to the York County Police Station and have mom arrested for taking our money. We left the house as if we were going to work but instead stuck to our plan. The police station had a small opening down from the front door. The desk cop asked us what we wanted, and I told him. He stood up and told us that he knew our mother. Just then, Mr. Amos Palmer (Rest in Peace) one of our local Black police officers came walking by and the desk cop told him what we wanted.

Mr. Amos said, "Does Miss Dot know you are down here trying to get her arrested?"

In unison, we said, "No."

Mabel felt inclined to tell him that it was all my idea. Mr. Amos told us to go straight home, and he would not tell our mom that we were at the police station trying to have her arrested. Thank God, he kept his word, or I may not have been able to write anybody's book.

Chapter 13

Time To Pay Up

ONE DAY THE DEVIL HIMSELF came by to see mom. He wanted her to drop the child support charges. Court was coming up soon. He pushed her against the front door and Aunt Jackie just happened to be looking out of her screen door. Aunt Jackie came outside and told William to get his ass on down the street somewhere. William had a few words to say. Aunt Jackie said, "William do not play with me. I am not Dorothy and I will fuck you up William (her words exactly)."

I am glad Aunt Jackie stepped in. Lord knows mom had many trials and tribulations with William. God's favor was always upon her. Dorothy was a praying mom and did not drop the charges.

When court came up, Mary, Mabel, and I went to court with mom. The judge told William he owed twenty-one thousand in back child support.

William yelled to the judge, "I'm not giving that bitch a damn dime."

That was not very smart. The judge said, "Bailiff, lock Mr. Smallwood up until he decides to pay his child support."

When the officer handcuffed and escorted him out of the courtroom, I felt somewhat sorry for him. We walked mom home, then we went to the York County Jail to see him, and they let us see him. William gave us his work number and Mary called his boss and told him what happened. His boss bailed him out, and he agreed to make payments to mom when they went back to court. He paid for a little while then stopped paying again.

Chapter 14

I Have A Secret

"A YEAR FILLED WITH TEENAGE EXPERIMENTATION with life, growing up too fast. Seeking independence from family controls to find one's own voice." (Marion Peterson-Fields, 2020)

Those times were very pivotal in forming lasting friendships. During that time, I met my best girlfriend, Cookie Peterson. I loved her and still today, more than 55 years later. We hung around together at my house or her house. We would sit around on my front porch. Cookie had a part-time job and always had her stash. I would sing with Joe and braid his hair sitting out front of our house while Cookie would try her hand at braiding Ronnie's hair when he was singing with Joe in my mom's house. Mom had her eye on him to because he was too old for Cookie, like Joseph was too old for me. I was one of his backup singers with Phyllis Montouth, Gwendolyn Pendarvis, and Sheila Drayden at different times. We thought we were all that in our white pleated skirts and white and green flowered tops. I was able to be alone with him many times. Phyllis would always tell Joseph to stop chasing me because he was too old.

One night I was out after curfew with him and you know what happened. He pressured me so hard with well-known lies that boys still use today. You cannot get pregnant the first time, it will not hurt I promise, (liar,) I will pull it out in time, so you will not get pregnant, (liar.) June, no period, and I am in panic mode. I told him my predicament when he came over. I was afraid to grow. I hardly ate anything. Joseph had a job working at the railroad station, loading potatoes off the train down by the old bus station in York, Pennsylvania where the baseball field is now located. We went to a doctor and I had a checkup. The doctor gave me vitamins, but I would not take them for I was afraid to grow. Lucky for me, everyone was wearing tent dresses, and I had plenty of them. Joseph's sister Jeanette was a booster, and she liked me a lot. She dressed me well. I did a good job of hiding it, but I knew I would not be able to hide it forever. Every time I saw Joseph, he asked me if I told my mom and I would say, "Hell no, you tell her." If I told her, that would have sealed my casket. Joseph was getting nervous. He was 18 years old and I was only 15 years old. That was not a good thing.

September of 1964. Joseph's mother, Leona Kearse, was murdered. Her boyfriend killed her. It happened in the backyard at their house on Green Street. Joseph and his siblings were so emotionally broken. Joseph was present when this incident occurred. He suffered a gunshot wound to his hand while trying to help his mom. He was in the hospital for several weeks.

He had a day pass from the hospital to attend his mother's funeral services. While he was in York Hospital, I took snacks to him after school. I walked from Hanna Penn to York Hospital every evening after school for eight or nine blocks. Mom actually gave me money to get snacks for him. He was worried about his hand. One of the surgeons told him they would have to amputate his right thumb and index finger.

Later, a young hand surgeon from Philadelphia, Pennsylvania came to examine him and told him he would save his thumb and index finger, but he could not remove the pellets from his hand. When released from the hospital, he took me to his mom's house to show me her jewelry and clothing, except there was nothing there. (Later he found out that one of his aunts took all of his mother's belongings.) I should have known that was a trap to get me alone. However, I was thinking as a teenager, not an educated woman, and he relied on that.

Thanksgiving came and went and Christmas break was looking me in the face. Joseph was now fearful of going to jail because he knew that if my mom found out that I was pregnant, he would be in trouble. He soon moved to Baltimore to stay with his Dad. Mom had warned me about Joseph Kearse too many times to count. Later I found out several other girls liked him to. Phyllis also told me there were two other teen girls pregnant to Joseph and one of them was her little sister. That rattled me a little, but Phyllis and I remained friends and until this day, we still are. I asked him about it, and he said that was not true.

Christmas break 1964 arrived. Mom was cooking her big dinner and baking all kinds of sweets while spinning records. In this house, we entered from the front door that opened into the living room, then the dining and then the kitchen. We had a wall phone between the dining room and kitchen. Mom and all of my siblings were present. It was a cheerful house for a while. The phone rang, and when that happened, everyone thought it was for him or her. Mabel got to the phone first answered it and yelled, "Lou it is for you."

Mom said, "Who is on the phone?" and Mabel said, "Her boyfriend Joe Kearse."

73

I was talking with him on that wall phone positioned between the kitchen and the dining room for some time. Each time Mom walked back and forth, past me between those doorways, she gave me the look of death.

About the fourth or fifth time she walked past me, she stopped and looked me in the face with a death stare and said, "You hussy, I know what is wrong with you. Are you pregnant Sandra Lee?"

I started crying, but that was not going to save me. Mom snatched that phone out of my hand and started beating me with it. Mom went crazy and was cussing and hitting me with that phone. Mom did not even know how to cuss.

Mary tried to intervene and said, "Mom you cannot be hitting a pregnant woman, you could go to jail."

Mom said, "Sit the hell down or you will get some too!"

Then she took a break from hitting me and started talking into the phone. "Joseph Kearse is that you on the phone?"

He must have answered for she continued her conversation with him. Her words exactly, "Joseph Kearse, if you do not want to be in jail with a ball and chain around your ankle, you better make it your business to get up here to explain to me how you intend to take care of your baby."

Joseph was living in Baltimore with his father William Kearse and his stepmother temporarily. That phone call was on Wednesday December 23, 1964. I knew mom was mentally broken for my sister Mary already had two children, Tracey and Bernard. This was going to be another financial burden on her.

The day after Christmas December 26, 1964, Joseph Kearse was at my house with cloth diapers, glass baby bottles of all sizes, baby clothes, carnation milk, and Karo syrup for baby formula. He gave my mom money for diaper service and told mom he would send me money every payday. He kept his word. Mom took me to York Hospital to the free clinic for mothers to get prenatal care, even though it was late in my pregnancy. While we were there that day, I overheard several white nurses talking about all the pregnant colored teenage girls coming for care. I was embarrassed; I knew it was a bad thing.

When mom and I were walking home from the York Hospital to our house after that appointment, I heard God talk to me as he did when I was a little girl dealing with William. I cannot explain it, but God has always come to me in visions, awake or asleep. I decided I was going to be okay. I knew mom was very disappointed, but I knew she was not going to kill me. I knew she was emotionally sick about me being pregnant.

It was about a month after she found out that I was pregnant, that she told me I was her dream. She wanted me to make it out of here. I knew my life was going to be a challenge, but I was going to find my way out. That drove me from that day on to thrive to be somebody more than just a black teenage mom from the ghetto. I told mom not to worry because I would make it out some day.

I was babysitting my niece, Tracey, and my nephew Bernard when my water broke. Mabel, Dottie Mae, Pokey, Bucky, and Bonita were all in school. Mary was not home at the time; she went to the corner store at Fisher's Market one morning to get a pack of cigarettes a few weeks ago and didn't return home, but mom didn't worry because she often left home and returned weeks later. Mom was at work. Water was dripping down my legs. I knew what that meant. She told me what to expect. I was not having any pain at that point, but I was scared. I put Tracey and Bernard in Mary's stroller and took them to Aunt Sis's house on Maple Street, which was about seven blocks away from where I lived. Aunt Sis called my mom's job and gave her a message. Aunt Sis sent me to the hospital in a taxi and kept the kids. Aunt Sis also called William and told him to come and get Tracey and Bernard because she could not keep them. Mom eventually got to the hospital and found me. I was having labor pains now. I was acting out. Shit! I never had a baby before.

Mom rolled up in my room, acting as if she was a crazy woman. Mom said; "Shut up, you were not hollering like that when you got that baby in there."

I was still hollering asking God to make the pain go away.

Mom said, "You can call for God all you want, but that pain is not going anywhere." The nurse kept coming in and talking to my mom. I told the nurse to get the doctor and pull that damn baby out of me. I was in super cuss mode. I did not give a damn who was hearing me. The nurse would not get the doctor. She kept trying to calm me down. Wetting my lips with ice and rubbing my arm. Every time a pain would come, I would start screaming again, only this time yelling for the doctor to come. The doctor finally came in to check me and said, "It is soon time Sandra." I was like, what the fuck? Get this baby out of me right now."

I started reverting to mom. "Mom help me please, I am sorry." She finally started acting like a mom who was no longer mad crazy at me. Trying to comfort me and acting like the nice mom I knew she could be.

Finally, I pushed my baby out. The doctor announced it was a girl. The nurse laid her on my breast and mom looked at her with the brightest smile. They took her away to clean her up. Then they brought her back to me. While I was in the hospital, I was trying to figure out what to name my baby. I decided to name her Billy Jo, after my sister Mary's white girlfriend. Mom came to visit that evening. I told her that I named her Billy Jo after Mary's friend. Mom said, "You had better not name that child somebody's Billy Jo. I mean it Sandra Lee."

I decided to name her Kimmy Jo before leaving the hospital. February 24, 1965 was a Wednesday. Kimmy Jo Kearse was born at eight months, a six pounder. I had heard that her half-brother, Joseph, was born December 1964 and the other girl lost her baby. I was released form York Hospital Sunday, February 28, 1965. Mom had a ride to pick me up. She asked me what I named the baby and I told her Kimmy Jo. Mom said that is cute, Kimberly Jo. I left it at that. I went back to York High on Monday. Mom took off from work for a few days and arranged for my grandma, Mabel Paul-Smallwood, to babysit for me.

That Monday evening after school, it was cold and snowing outside, I took a taxicab to William's house because I wanted to get Tracey and Bernard back from William. I left a message for mom with Mabel as to where I was going. On my arrival to his house, his girlfriend Sarah and her two sisters were there. I told Sarah I wanted to get the kids and she said no way, your dad is not here, and he told me to keep the kids. I told her I would not leave without them. She and her sisters were making fun of me and saying negative things. I was very quiet and thinking to myself *you, bitches think you have me cornered but I am not leaving without my niece and nephew.* I was just sitting in a side chair and holding Tracey. Tracey was very hot to touch and had bumps and pus all over her. Bernard was in a playpen sitting with a bottle at two years old he did not need a bottle and was not on one at our house. About an hour later, there was a loud knock on the door and when Sarah opened, it was my mom. She walked in as if she was mafia mom. She said to Sarah, you got my daughter out here in the cold weather trying to get something that belongs to us, "Give me my grandkids right now." Mom took her coat off and wrapped Tracey up in it and gave her to me, then she took a blanket out of the playpen and wrapped Bernard in it, we walked out of the front door to a car she had waiting for us. The car ride home was mom talking and telling me I had no business being out in that weather after recently having a baby. She said this child got the chicken pox and these dumb ass people done put Vaseline all over her just made her more miserable.

Six weeks later, it was time for my post-natal appointment. The doctor wanted to put me on some type of birth control, but mom said no way. I heard those gadgets you put inside of these young girls could cause cancer. There was no birth control for me. One would think that mom would have elected for me to be on some type of birth control. After all, she had seven children with no birth control. She was the parent; I was a child with no say one way or the other. My babysitting arrangement worked out until the school year was over. I did not go back to school for eleventh grade because Grandma Mabel Paul did not want to babysit anymore. It was too much for her. We were moving again to East College Avenue a very large house. It was nice because our house was too small for mom, her children, and her grandchildren. In addition, I was pregnant again and mom did not know it yet. I confided in Mary and she said mom is going to kill you. I agreed with her. I knew I had to tell her and sooner than later.

I had missed my period two months before and Mary and my cousin Brenda talked me into having an abortion. They were the doctors. I agreed because I was afraid of mom. I had to go to Mary's room and wait for her and my cousin to come back from the store with the medicine I needed to take so my period would start. It seemed like forever, but finally they returned. Mary came back with a brown bag (Mom was at the bar cooking that evening). She took out a small can of ginger spice and a small plastic bottle of turpentine. She also had a pint of gin. The turpentine bottle had a black skeleton head on it and the bottle said poison. I told Mary that the turpentine would kill me -- a human person is not supposed to drink it. Mary told me I was stupid and was not going to die. I should trust her because she did this before. She told me to go make a pot of black coffee and bring it and a cup to her room. When I returned to her room, she was waiting. Mary poured a full cup of black coffee for me. She got a shot glass. She put a teaspoon of ginger in the shot glass. Then she added a small amount of the turpentine and gin, mixed it, and told me to drink it down as fast as I could then drink the coffee behind it. I was gagging trying to get it down. I drank all of the coffee. Mary gave me another cup of hot black coffee. I kept gagging. Mary yelled you had better not vomit. I could not feel anything in my stomach. About an hour or two later I started getting cramps so bad, I thought I was dying. I was groaning. Mary told me to shut up. Mary took some plastic, some rags, and an old sheet and made a bed for me on the floor. She said if mom ever found that mattress with blood all over it, I would not be able to explain it. Sometime through the night, I woke up with blood everywhere. I balled up the sheet and put it between my legs. I went to Mary's room right across from mine and woke her up. I was frantic. I told her I was bleeding to death, and we have to call an ambulance. She told me to calm down; I was not dying. I did not die, obviously. That was an ordeal, but my period came on and I was happy as a child in a candy store.

Two months later, I was in the same situation because Joseph told me I could not get pregnant for two months after having a baby. I did not tell Mary because I did not want her to give me another abortion.

Just the thought of that gin, turpentine, and ginger made me vomit. I hate ginger and gin to this day.

Summer, July nineteen hundred and sixty five was going well it seemed like all of my teenage girlfriends had babies or were having babies. Kimmy Jo was five months old. I was leaving the house one day to go to Penn Park to hang out. I dressed Kimmy Jo in her outfit, got my stroller out, and was ready to leave when mom intervened and said, "Just where do you think you are going young lady?"

I responded, "To Penn Park to watch the drill team practice."

She said, "You might be going to watch the drill team practice, but Kimberly Jo will not be going with you. Kimberly Jo is five months old; she is not going with you to anybody's park for something to happen to her."

I had a flash back to when Kimmy Jo was born in that delivery room. Mom claimed her that day. I said, "Mom, all of the girls take their babies with them to the park."

She said, "I am not their mom." I was so mad at her, thinking she owned Kimmy Jo. I ran away to Aunt Sis' house on Maple Street. Every time I was mad at mom because she would not let me take Kimmy Jo to the park with me, I would go to Aunt Sis' house. I found out later that Aunt Sis called mom and told her I was there every time. Tattle tale!

I was not going to school the upcoming year (eleventh grade), so I thought it was just as good a time as any to tell mom I was pregnant again. Yes, I was now a teenage, high-school dropout with a baby and another baby on the way. Tent dresses were no longer in style. There was no way I could hide it from her, especially since she saw me close up every day since I was not attending school that year. It was a warm

September evening when she came home from work. I waited for her to change out of her work clothes. I wanted to tell her before she found out that two of my other sisters were pregnant as well. She sat down to have a cold beer. She always liked beer. I sat down in a chair by her, while holding Kimmy Jo. I figured she was not going to slam me with Kimmy Jo sitting on my lap.

Mom looked at me and said, "What Sandra Lee? What do you want?"

I said, "Nothing."

She said, "Do you want a beer?"

I said, "No. I do not like beer."

She said, "I know. Therefore, what do you want?"

I said, "I am pregnant." Mom sat up straight and swallowed the rest of her beer in one swallow. I did not know what she was thinking, but I knew it was not good. Actually, now that I was thinking about it, it was kind of her fault. She had seven children and she knew that it was not easy to stop having intercourse once one started, especially if birth control methods were not an option on the table. Mom is the one who would not give permission for me to have birth control. I bet she was thinking about that birth control now.

Chapter 15

Joseph Kearse Is Going to Jail

WE WERE NOW LIVING ON East College Avenue. Mom finally has her own bedroom. I was so happy that she could now have real privacy. The bedroom had a nice closet. Mom soon went to the Salvation Army and found an old wooden bedroom set with a bed and a dresser that she cleaned up and made look like new. It was a roomy house. There was a living room, dining room, and kitchen on the first floor. There were three bedrooms on the second floor and two bedrooms on the third floor. Wow, we had space. Things were hectic because all of mom's children were now teenagers, except Bonita and Bucky. Several grandchildren lived in the house. Everyone was acting out except me. Pokey thought she would try running away and she did that on more than one occasion. Mom did not say much when she did not come home on those occasions because she found out she was with her boyfriend, Rock Mitchell.

Mom looked at me and said, "Wherever your sister is, when they get tired of feeding her, she will be back." Usually by the next evening, Pokey would be back at home. Yes, mom whupped her butt. Pokey was always doing something, like stealing my clothes and shoes from the house. I had so much because Jeanette Kearse, Joseph's sister, always kept me looking good. Mom did not make me give them back; she wanted to but never pushed it.

One day when Pokey asked to wear one of my dresses; I told her no way and mom chimed in and said, "Yes, she can wear it. You have more than enough clothing."

I was so irritated with Pokey. I told mom that she is going to ruin my dress; you know how careless she is. Well when she returned home, my dress ruined with grass stains all over it. That is why I did not want her to wear the dress, because I loaned her a dress prior to this time and she did not take care of it. It is a long story.

Bucky and Bonita were always good little kids. Pokey was always into something and she was the best storyteller. I always brought clothing for Bucky and Bonita. I would dress them with matching shorts and tops as if they were twins. They looked just like twins with their blond hair and green/gray eyes. I always had money from Joseph. Mary was Mary, home off and on. Dottie Mae and Mabel always hooked school.

One fall afternoon they decided to run around and pull false fire alarms. I guess they liked seeing the news about someone pulling those alarms. It was happening for three days. Mom was watching the news one evening and said, "It does not make any damn sense that someone would do such a thing." I told Mom they should put them in a detention center when they find them and make their parents pay a big fine.

The next morning the news reported that they had received a clue that the perpetrators were two females, a colored tall girl, and a white midget girl. A few hours later on a Friday evening, a police officer knocked on our front door to talk to mom. The police wanted to talk to Dottie Mae; they knew mom had a midget daughter that looked like she was a white girl. Under house interrogation, Dottie Mae caved, started crying, and told on Mabel. Mabel gave her the look of death and Dottie Mae told Mabel she did not want to go to jail. They all took a ride to the police station and in a few hours, they were home again. The police officer gave them a ride back home. They received a pass, no probation just an insignificant punishment. Thanks to Uncle Billy Smallwood who was a York, County Police Officer (Rest in Peace) at that time. I did not know what punishment they would receive from mom, but I knew it would be coming. Both sent upstairs after dinner and told not to come down until she told them to. Thinking to myself, as I did all the time when I was a teen, if she does not beat their butts, she has lost control.

The next day, Saturday morning, she had a field day whupping their behinds. Mary, Pokey, Bonita, Bucky, and I were downstairs listening to all of the commotion. When it was all over, mom came downstairs and was in a snapping mode, "Do you all have something to do?" We cleared the living room so fast. Those two weeks of not being able to go out after school was painful for Mabel and Dottie Mae. Mom was getting tired of Mabel, Dottie Mae, and Pokey acting out. All three of them were always into something. If it was not school, it was something else. The principal at Hannah Penn Junior High sent mom a letter informing her that the school administration was going to expel Mabel and Dottie Mae from school because they were such troublemakers. They gave her a choice to sign them out of school or they would expel them. She signed them both out of school. Pokey was doing better in school with Mabel and Dottie Mae separated from her. Pokey was still acting out away from school.

Joseph was now living back in York. I saw him on a regular and mom knew that. When he came by to see me one evening, mom was home. I had not told Joseph that I was pregnant again. However, he was going to find out now. He knocked on the door and I went to let him in. Mom yelled from the kitchen, "Is that Joe?" I said, "Yes, it is." Joseph and I walked to the front room and mom met us there.

Mom said, "Take a seat young man." He did and so did I.

She asked him if he knew I was pregnant and he said, "No, Miss Dot." She gave Joseph a choice to either marry me or go to jail. She said, "You do not have to marry her. You can go to jail for statutory rape if you choose to."

He said, "Miss Dot, I didn't rape Lou!"

She said, "How old are you?"

He said, "Nineteen."

She said, "How old is Sandra Lee?"

He said, "Sixteen."

"I ask you again, do you plan to marry my daughter or go to jail?" She looked dead in his eyes and said, "I didn't hear you."

He said, "I guess I am going to marry her." I later told my mom that I did not want to get married because there was another boy talking to me.

Mom said, "Dammit Sandra Lee! (She always said Sandra Lee when she was mad). You should have thought about that before you started playing house with Mr. Kearse."

We set a date for November 1965. It did not matter what Joseph and I wanted. It was a done deal. The date was set and invitations sent. We were supposed to go to Baltimore to be married, return, and have our wedding party at my mom's house on East College Avenue. The event was to start at 5:00 PM on a Saturday evening. That morning, Joseph's Sister Jeanette came by and told my mom that Joe was in jail for child support.

Mom said, "What! Joseph has another child?" Moreover, Jeanette told her he did. Mom did not know that, but I did.

If mom knew there was a third girl pregnant to Joseph, she would have killed Joseph right on the spot. His son's mama had him arrested for child support. I heard later that her mom made her do it. He was in jail since Friday evening after he got off work. Mom was mad as hell. Mom is now calling Jesus, saying Lord Jesus, Lord Jesus. My mom and I were in a panic mode. My mom got a ride to William's house and told him the situation. She told me later that she asked him to bail Joseph out because he had never really done much for me, and he must have felt bad about it, as he did bail Joseph out of jail. He took him home to get his clothes and then brought him to our house on East College Avenue.

When Joseph entered our house, mom asked him "How old is that girl young man? She repeated, "How old is she? Who put you in jail for child support yesterday?"

He just looked at her; by now, I was crying. Mom told Joseph to go upstairs, get dressed and for him and me to act happy like we were just married. She said we would go to Baltimore next week to get married; the date was no big deal. I did not know how we were supposed to pull that off. I was sixteen years old and he was nineteen years old, and we were never married before.

That evening guests started to roll in. People were congratulating us with hugs and kisses. Mom had food galore, and she made a beautiful

86

cake. She sure knew how to fake it. After a while, it seemed real. Joseph and I were playing the part, smiling, dancing, and having a great time. I guess Joseph was smiling because he was not in the York County Jail. He was enjoying his freedom for the moment. The end of the celebration came upon us. Joseph, mom, and I opened all of our gifts. I cannot remember what we received. So to all of you York residents who came to that wedding way back in 1966, sorry I am not able to return gifts because I have no idea what they were or where they are. Time went on and we never did go to get married that next week or any other week after that. We just lived the lie.

February 22, 1966 my second child, a boy, Kevin Scott came along. The painful memory from less than a year ago popped into my head. Mom was home when I went into labor. She sent me to York Hospital in a Taxi, and she came a little later. Hell yes, I was in the crazy, hollering cuss mode like I experienced the previous year giving birth to Kimmy Jo. Mom showed up and gave me a look, but I did not fear her this time. Every time a pain came, I let the whole York Hospital know I was not going to pretend I was not in pain. They did not let me stay in labor to long because the baby was not engaging the way it was supposed to do. Kevin would not turn headfirst. The doctor spoke with my mom and told her they wanted to do a saddle block to calm me down. I did not know what that meant. When it was over, all of the pain went away. I was happy as all get out. I did not have to push no more. Pain was gone. I even struck up a conversation with the doctor and the nurses. The doctor had to cut me to widen the space to get Kevin out. He was not breathing on delivery.

My mom was asking what was wrong. The nurse said nothing, and they just wanted to warm him up. I could see them suctioning him with the bubble syringe. He was so yellow (jaundiced). I received seventy-five stitches when birthing him. I know that because I ask the

87

doctor and he said we are at seventy-five stitches; we are not counting any longer, Sandra. He was a seven-and-a half pounder. When the doctor discharged me from the hospital, Kevin Scott, (I named him Kevin because Joseph other son's name was Joseph) had to stay for a week or so, until he was better. When I arrived home, I could barely walk because of all the stitches and the pain. The warm sitz baths I had to do every three hours or so was comforting. I could not lift Kimmy Jo because of the stitches and the pain. That was convenient for mom; she loved keeping Kimmy Jo with her. I did not know how I was going to get my children from her when I was ready to leave.

Finally, Kevin was able to come home. Mom went to pick him up with a friend of hers. I had to stay upstairs in my room with him for a week or so. The stairs were still too much for me to maneuver. This one afternoon, Kimmy Jo was in my room with her baby brother and me. She was sitting on the floor. I told her I was going to the bathroom and I would be right back. I put Kevin in the drawer on the floor (makeshift bassinet). I was gone only a few minutes to pee. I shuffled back quickly and found Kimmy Jo with a pillow she had taken from my bed, smothering Kevin. I am like, "No, No, No Kimmy Jo. You will hurt the baby!" I guess I yelled so loud that I frightened Kimmy Jo. She started crying her little heart out and hugging me. Mom came up to see what all the fuss was about and I told her. Mom told me I had to involve Kimmy Jo with all that I could so she would not feel left out. I would let her hold his bottle, hold him on her lap when she was in the room with me, and pat him on the back when I burped him. I never left her alone again with Kevin after that. I guess jealousy is innate. No way at age, one a child could know to smother and kill a baby. Lord Jesus. That was a narrow escape. I was on guard after that incident. At my six-week post-natal examination mom finally agreed for me to be on birth control via and IUD (Intrauterine device).

My Grandmom Mabel Smallwood and Aunt Sis came to see Kevin a couple of days after he came home. Grandmom Mabel told my mom that there was no way that was any Joe Kearse baby because he was too light. Mom reminded Grandmom Mable that babies birth color is not the color they will be. Mom believed Kevin had Joe's eyes. My maternal grandmother came to visit us on East College soon after Kevin Scott was born also. Her visit was especially nice to see her newest great grandchild. Nanny came through the back door with Uncle Charles. She had a difficult time stepping up on the porch. Mom asked her if she was all right. Nanny responded Dorothy I am okay, just a little tired today. Two weeks later, March 1966, my Nanny passed away. We were all so terribly hurt to the core, and it really broke my mom and Aunt Almeda down. After the funeral was over, mom decided that she needed space to find herself. She was a little down because now I am not the only teen mom in the house causing her further financial burdens.

One-day mom was on her way to work. Before she left the house, she told Mary that there was a can of sweet corn in the kitchen and she wanted her to heat it for Bucky and Bonita's lunch. After mom, left, Mary walked down to the corner store on College Avenue and George Street and bought some butterscotch krimpets and an apple pie for her and me. When she arrived back from the store, she and I started to watch television and chill with our snacks and soda. In the meantime, Mabel came downstairs and went into the kitchen. We did not pay her any mind. Soon Mary thought she smelled the aroma of corn and asked me if I smelled the corn, which I did and nodded, *yes*. Mary stood up and walked into the kitchen. I heard all of the commotion and went to see what was going on.

Mary told Mabel that mom told her to use the can of corn for Bucky and Bonita's lunch. Mabel told Mary that she bought that corn yesterday. Mary told Mabel that it would be over her dead body if she thought she was going to eat that corn. Well, Mary was not playing. Mabel was stirring the corn adding butter and rolling her eyes. Mary walked around her and spit in the corn. Mabel picked up the pan of corn off the stove and smacked Mary in the face. Corn flew all over the kitchen walls and the floor. It was on then. I got out of their way; you know I just had my baby boy, and I was not trying to get between them. They fought from the kitchen to the living room. They stopped for a few minutes, both huffing and puffing several times. I thought that was my clue to tell them what time mom would be coming home from work. It took them about two hours to get the house back together. They had everything in place. Mom came home on time and we were all chilling in the living room watching television. Mom never found out about that can of corn. Mary fed Bucky and Bonita toasted English muffins with butter and grape jelly for lunch that afternoon. That was one of those hard times, when food was scarce in our house. Mabel swears to this day that she purchased the can of corn. Mary swears that she was lying

Our Grandmom Margaret McGee and her husband Mr. Charlie McGee would come over to visit from Columbia, Pennsylvania once a month or so and give us all kinds of day-old pastries and bread. Mr. McGee worked at a grocery food store in Columbia, Pennsylvania.

Mom did date but nothing serious. One day a man stopped by and I knew I had seen him sometime in my life before but could not place where. Mom told me his name was Mr. Bill Duncan, and I remembered him from when I was little girl back on 480 Codorus Street. I remember when I used to call him collect to tell him when William was beating mom. He was a long-haul truck driver like my Dad. That is how I knew him. He ran into my Mom at a local bar where she was the cook. He started coming by often but never spent the night. Mom had her own bedroom now, so she could have let him spend the night. I asked her about it one evening. She reminded me that, "No man should spend the night in your house unless you are serious about him.

Chapter 16

Moving to Baltimore Maryland
2559 Hollins Avenue

SPRING 1966, MOM DECIDED SHE was done with York and decided to follow Mr. Bill Duncan to Baltimore, Maryland. By this time, all of the girls except Bonita had a baby or was pregnant and doing what they wanted to do. Dottie Mae had been pregnant, but she could never carry the baby. The doctors said she was too small. It was time for mom to free herself from us wanting-to-be grownups with kids. Mom needed to get away from all of this. She had no breaks from taking care of all of her grandchildren and us. My siblings and I were living on East College Avenue with Mom at that time. We had to make plans as to where everyone was going.

Mary and Mabel went to live with their boyfriends and Dottie Mae, Pokey and Bonita went to stay with William until mom settled in Baltimore. Bucky stayed with me. Joseph found a house for us. He found a small house up behind Maple Street across from the old Chrispus Attucks Recreation Center. Things were going okay, but I had never been separated from my mom or my siblings. One summer evening Kevin had a crying fit. I tried everything mom taught me to get him to stop crying. I made sure that a safety pin had not opened in his diaper. I burped him, rocked him, and patted him on my shoulder. I walked around, singing to him and nothing worked. Finally, I put him in his crib put a pillow behind his back and a small one in front of him so he could not choke. I took Kimmy Jo by the hand and my niece Tracey downstairs to sit on the front porch. You know how black folk are. Everybody was walking past and looking at us on the porch. I blocked out his crying. Soon Tracey asked me if she could sneak upstairs to see if Kevin was sleeping. I let her. Tracey came back down and said, "Aunt Sandi, the baby is sleeping now." At that point, I knew I needed to be with my mom. I was going to plan to get the heck out of York.

It was hard not having my mom around; In addition, I could not handle Bucky. He and his play brother Wayne Wilson were hooking school every day I went up to the school and found out that Bucky and Wayne were out of school more days than they were in school for the semester. The principal said that the next time they were out of school he would suspend them. Well they would have loved that. They were running around downtown all day during the school hours.

One day they took it upon themselves to break into New Way Cleaners on West College Avenue on a Sunday morning. The silent alarm went off once they got inside. The police came and caught them red-handed. They both received a free ride to the York City Police department from Mr. Amos Palmer who took responsibility for them and brought them home to me. It was time for mom to come and get her son. I called her and she came the following weekend to pick him up and take him with her.

Summer was approaching, and I wanted to finish school. It was torture separated from my mom. In addition, being a mom and playing wife was just too much for a sixteen-year-old girl. By the end of July,

I really wanted to see my mom. The phone number I had used to contact her in the past was no longer working. I decided I would go to Baltimore to find her. I knew she lived on Hollins Avenue. That is all I had to go on.

One Friday evening, Joseph came home from work and I told him I was going to Baltimore to find my mom. I used the house money to purchase a Greyhound bus ticket the prior week. He asked me whom I was going to get to watch the kids. I told him he had to watch the kids because they were his kids too, and he agreed I should go. Kevin was five months old and Kimmy Jo was a year and five months of age. Joseph was worried because they were so little. I told him I would be back in two days. I left on a Friday evening and the plan was for me to return on Sunday morning. I had a round trip ticket.

He said, "What about Kevin, he cries all the time?"

I said, "Rock him on your lap. Pat him on his back. Walk around and sing to him as I do. He will soon stop and go to sleep." Inside my head I was thinking, *it is your turn Joseph.*

When I arrived in Baltimore at the Greyhound bus station, I was a little afraid. The bus station was so big, and I never seen so many colored people. I went outside (I had no bags) and saw people waving at taxis and plain cars. I found out quickly that the plain cars were like taxis. Men were hustling to make a living. I stood in front of the building for a little while and a cab driver pulled over to me. He asked me if I needed help. I told him I was looking for my mom and that I knew she lived on Hollins Avenue, but I did not have an address. He asked me where I was coming from and I told him York, Pennsylvania. He told me to go inside the bus station and wait for him to come back. He needed to make a little more money before he quit for the evening. He came back to look for me in about two hours, as he said he would. I was a little worried, but the Holy Spirit told me to trust him and I did. We went outside to his taxicab. I sat in the back. He told me Hollins Avenue was a very short street. He drove what seemed like forever to me, which was probably because I was nervous. It was hot, the cab windows were down, kids filled the streets, and people were sitting on their porches while kids were skating in the streets holding and blasting their radios. People were blasting the song Function at the Junction on the radios by Shorty Long. Then out of nowhere, I saw a little boy skating passed us. I yelled out of the taxi window to my brother, "Bucky! Bucky!" It was dark outside, but I knew it was my little brother. We pulled up beside him and he stopped. The cab driver put the inside cab light on, and he saw me. I opened the car door and he started hugging me saying, "Come on Lou, we have to go to mom." I had a few more dollars, and I offered it to the taxicab driver. He would not take it. He said; "I am glad you are safe."

Bucky took me to a row house that was across the street from a bar where the music was blasting out of the windows. I followed Bucky through the vestibule to the kitchen where mom, Mr. Bill and another woman was sitting. (That woman would later become my legal guardian.)

I said, "Hey mom."

Mom responded, "What are you doing here?"

I said, "Looking for you." She stood up, hugged me, and introduced me to the woman, Miss Bernice Owens. Miss Bernice had a daughter, Portia, and a son, James, who we called Jimmy; they both became siblings to me. I loved them like my own siblings. Mom and Mr. Bill at that time were staying across the street with a friend that Mr. Bill knew.

I stayed with mom that night and went home the next afternoon, which was Saturday. I thought Joseph might be having a hard time with the kids. While I was there, I told her I wanted to go back to school. She said I could not stay with her because she did not have her own place but was working on it and that I could come then. I went back home feeling good about seeing my mom. Now I will be able to tell my sisters that I saw her, and she is safe with Mr. Bill.

About two weeks later, I received a letter from mom. She wrote that the friend she and Mr. Bill were living with told them to get out and that Miss Bernice, whom I meant while I was in Baltimore, said she could live with her. She also told me that Tracey, Kimmy Jo, Kevin and I could come there too, but not Joseph. That was good; I was tired of playing wife with all the wife responsibilities that went along with being a wife when we were not married anyways. I knew my mom would help with the kids. Mr. Bill rented a room in a rooming house for the time being.

Chapter 17

Generational Curses

I PACKED UP MY KIDS, ALONG with my niece, Tracey, whom I stole from Mary's backyard when she was four. I knew Mary was in an abusive relationship with her husband, Clabber Richardson, and he was beating her regularly. I would go to see her and see where she was using makeup to hide her bruises, just as mom did when we were little kids. At the time, we did not know the generational curse of abuse would affect us all in one way or another. I was always worried about Tracey. Bernard was now back living with William.

Early one Saturday morning I asked Joseph to keep an eye on Kimmy Jo and Kevin Scott while I walked over across the bridge to Green Street to check on Mary. When I arrived, I saw Tracey sitting on the back porch, top step with her head down and her hands folded on her lap. I called to her and she just looked at me and did not talk. She was about twenty steps from me, and the fence was about three feet tall. The street was quiet, and no one was out. I told her to come to me and she said, "I am not supposed to move from this spot or Clabber will beat me again."

I was on fire inside for Tracey; I loved her so very much. I told her to come to me and she would not move. I went around the corner to the store on Princess Street and brought some penny candy. I went back to the yard and convinced Tracey to come to get the candy from me. I told her if she ran to me fast, she could get back and Clabber would not know that she moved. She ran down the three steps quickly and when she reached me, I snatched her up over that fence, put her on my back, and ran like hell. She was just four years old. How anyone could beat a child like this? Tracey had two black eyes, old and new bruises all over her little body. I went straight to the York Hospital Emergency Room to have her examined for any broken bones. The doctors wanted to know what happened to her and she told them Clabber beat her for being bad. The doctor wanted to know if she was going back to her mom, and I told him no.

Later that evening, Mary and Clabber drove to my house. I was sitting on the front porch with Joseph. Mary got out of the car and asked me if I had Tracey and I told her that I did. She asked for her, and I told her she could not have her.

Mary said to me, "Sandra, she is my daughter." and I said, "She is not Clabber Richardson's daughter."

Now Clabber is out of the car approaching the front porch. I stand up and say to Mary, "If you do not want him to go to jail, leave now because I took Tracey to the hospital and they have documentation that your fucking boyfriend beat her."

Joseph walked out of our front door, stood up in front of me, and told Clabber it was a good time for both of them to leave. Reluctantly, they both got into the car and left. They never came back nor did they call the police. I believe that Mary was relieved that Joseph and I had her daughter. In spite of that, we stayed sisters and talked much after that. Mary was okay with me having Tracey for the time being. I will always believe that my sister wanted rescuing too; however, she did not know how to find her way out of the abusive situation she had fallen into.

I took my kids and our clothes and got a Greyhound Bus to Baltimore, just in time to start eleventh grade. I left Joseph to clear out the house and resign from his job. He soon came to Baltimore and lived with his Dad (William Kearse) and stepmother. I started eleventh grade positively raring to go. School was going good, after I became acclimated to the 'yes ma'am 'and 'no sir' code in the Baltimore City school system. I learned fast. In class, the teacher was taking attendance, roll call. He would call a student's names and they would say, "Sir." When he got to my name, it was almost at the end of the roster, being a Smallwood from York where we did not say Sir and Ma'am to the teachers. He said, "Sandra Smallwood." I said, "Present," as we did at York High. He said, "Are you new here?" I responded, "Yes." He said, "Yes what." Well after a few visits to the principal's office and notes being sent home, I started thinking about how I was going to deal with the teachers in the Baltimore school system. I decided that it was going to be a long two years if I did not conform to the school standard. All I could think about was the slave and master control. At Miss Bernice's house, Portia and her brother had to say yes ma'am to mom Bernice. It was the norm, so I conformed at home also.

Mom was trying hard to find a house because she wanted to get her other kids from York. Miss Bernice told her she could bring her kids if she wanted too. Mom told her that she had many kids. Miss Bernice told her it was okay and that we would make it work. Bonita, Pokey, and Mabel came to Baltimore soon. Mary and Dottie Mae did not. Mabel later decided that she did not like Baltimore and went back to York. They did visit though. Mom and Mr. Bill found a house across the street from Miss Bernice, so I did not have to change schools. Mom and some of her kids were together again. Mom found a day job in a hospital laundry department and soon brought her father, Charles Jackson from York to live with us. He was living in a boarding house in York. Miss Bernice was a nurse and worked nights. She took care of Kimmy Jo, Kevin and Tracey while mom worked and I attended school.

June 16, 1967 my grandpop Charles Jackson died from a stroke. Bucky was so sad. He and grandpop were inseparable. That was very hard for mom. Her sister Aunt Almeda came from Lancaster for his funeral. I remember my Grandpop's body lying in a casket in Miss Bernice's House for three days before the funeral. We all got through that. I will never forget the day of his death for it was two days after my birthday. I made it through eleventh grade, and I am not pregnant. Remember back in nineteen hundred and sixty six mom agreed that I cloud be on some type of birth control plan. Soon I started losing weight and I could not eat; I was so sick. Mom was so worried. She told Miss Bernice about it and she advised mom to take me to the hospital where she worked at South Baltimore General Hospital. Mr. Bill drove us to the hospital. I was examined and the IUD (inter uterine device) had to be removed from my uterine tubes. It caused an infection. Birth control pills were not around yet and Joseph did not use condoms. Recovery went well.

Portia and I hit it off from the start. She always said I was the big sister she never had. She used to sneak and wear my clothes to school. I would catch her many times. I told her to ask me the next time. Portia and I joined the youth choir at Shiloh Christian Community Church. The whole neighborhood was involved in the choir. We went to rehearsals at the Church on Saturdays. We traveled many places to perform at different churches. We sang somewhere one time and my sister Portia (I was now calling her sister) got happy and the choir director Mr. Lane gave me a stare. I did not know what he wanted me to do about it. Portia got carried away shouting and lost it for a little bit. I teased her as well. We laugh about it still today. Mr. Lane used to let the entire choir member group hang out at his house and play games. They all knew I had children and they embraced me in spite of that. It was fantastic having somewhere safe to go for good, clean fun and being accepted.

Mabel came down in the summer and hung with us at times. We went to parties, wore awesome clothes and we were hot! Neighborhood boys started asking Portia about Mabel and me. She told them we were her sisters from Pennsylvania. We formed our own singing trio and captured the attention of the local kids while singing on our front porch. Joseph lived on the other side of town. I saw him less. He came one day and saw a boy who was hanging around me. His name was Ludie and he lived in the next block. He liked me and he took me to meet his mom and dad one summer evening. They liked my kids and me. I had them with me. They were okay with the two of us being friends. Joseph was not. One evening Joseph came over to my mom's house to see me. She was at work. He asked me about Ludie. I told him he was just a friend from school. He started pulling me by my arm. I kept pulling away. He got so angry and started punching me in my face and to my body. He was hitting me everywhere and so fast. I did not have time to cry. I was sniffling somewhat when he was done. I was about a size eight. After he beat me, he tried to hug me. Who does that? It took me back to seeing my dad William beating my mom when I was a little girl. Kimmy Jo was crying, saying do not hit mommy. I held my two kids and in a short time, the tears came; I was crying and saying to myself, *I cannot do this.* Mom came home after work and asked what happened to me. I told her Joseph beat me up because he saw me talking to a neighborhood boy. Mom was furious. I had two black eyes, a busted lip and my sides were hurting from the beating. Now I really knew what mom went through when William was beating up on her. Mom wanted to have him arrested and I begged her not to. I wanted her to give him another chance. Against her better judgement, she did not call the police. It was summer; I stayed in the house until I looked a little better. I did not tell Portia what happened, but I knew mom told Miss Bernice.

Summer nineteen hundred and sixty seven, mom and Mr. Bill decided to move back to York because Mr. Bill found a better paying job. Mom arranged for me to stay with Miss Bernice Owens. They had to do legal guardian paperwork for me to stay in the state of Maryland. The guardianship paperwork was completed before mom left the city of Baltimore, Maryland. I soon started to call Miss Bernice mom Bernice. Mom was worried about leaving me in Baltimore with Joseph nearby. Mom Bernice took care of that. She told my mom not to worry about me because I was her daughter now. Joseph did not visit me unless mom Bernice was home. He had to call first before he came to visit.

My mom left with my siblings and Tracey to go back to York, Pennsylvania. Portia and I became very close once we were together so much. One night about two am in the morning, she was on the phone talking to her boyfriend, Ronnie Summerville, for hours. Mom Bernice had the operator cut into the call and tell her to hang up because she was trying to call us. Portia ran to my bedside in a panic, waking me up from a deep sleep.

"Saundra, mama is going to call."

Portia always called me Saundra. I guess it was a Baltimore thing. I said; "Call me for what?"

Portia knew she was in trouble for being on the phone that time in the morning. She wanted me to answer the phone for her because she felt that mom Bernice would not beat me because I was not her real daughter. I told her that I did not want to be in trouble. Portia was crying now. She said she would pay me back. I agreed to answer the phone when it rang, and it finally did ring. I answered it and mom Bernice was mad as all get-out. She wanted to know who was on the phone this time in the morning for over two hours with me. As agreed, I told her that I had been on the phone. Mom Bernice was yelling for a while. She asked if everything was okay, and I told her everything was fine. When she came home about eight in the morning from work, she came straight to me. I received a few whacks, but I could handle it. It was nothing like I got from my dad back in the day. I never told on Portia. She never got the opportunity to pay me back because I was not trying to get into any trouble.

September, nineteen hundred and sixty seven was the beginning of a new school year. Whew, I finally made it to twelfth grade. I was doing well. The school had a career day for seniors, and I attended it. I told a counselor that I wanted to be a nurse (mom Bernice influenced me so much, she was a nurse) and she told me I could never be a nurse because I was taking general classes instead of college prep classes in school. I felt some kind of way while riding the bus home from school. I cried on mom Bernice's shoulders. I explained to her what the counselor said. Her words exactly were, "Saundra, do not listen to everything you hear from counselors at your school. She said white or black. The white counselors make it their duty to keep black kids from college and the black counselors want to fit in so they do the same thing." Her words influenced me tremendously. I learned that day that one has to fight for what they want and believe in.

Thanksgiving and Christmas came and went. January arrived and while I was in school, I fainted while walking through the hallway to my next class. When I woke up, I was with the nurse. I looked puzzled but she did not. She asked, "Are you pregnant?"

I said, "I do not think I am pregnant." I started crying and saying if I am pregnant, I will not be able to finish school. The nurse said, "Yes you will, sweetheart. I will write a note for you to give to your mom. The note will explain how you may remain in school."

I gave the note to mom Bernice when I arrived home. The next day she took me to a clinic to have a pregnancy test done. Mom Bernice did not have to do that. After two pregnancies, in my heart I knew I was indeed pregnant with baby number three and the test confirmed it. I asked her in the clinic if I had to go back to York. She said not unless I wanted to.

Mom Bernice was in love with and attached to my son, Kevin; she did not want me to take him anywhere. God was always protecting my mom and me, always present in our lives and the lives of my siblings. Luckily, I was grateful to not be kicked out of mom Bernice's house, and sent back to York with my mom. Mom Bernice enrolled me in the school for unwed pregnant teens the following Monday. I called Joseph that evening and he came over to visit me. I told him I was pregnant again. This time, we did end up getting married. He promised to never ever, hit me again and I believed him. We married just before Karmentrina Schevelle Kearse delivered on March 15, 1968. We kept the secret to ourselves. It was no big deal because everyone in York thought we were already married. It was an easy birth. Karmentrina slid out with eyes wide open while sucking her thumb. She had a serious full head of hair, an afro right in style for 1968. No labor pains. I had some pressure and I asked the nurse if I could go to the bathroom and she said I could go in the bed. I said, "It is more than pee." The Sister said it was okay. (Born in a Catholic Hospital – Bon Secours in Baltimore, City)

"You can go in the bed." The doctor soon came in looked between my legs and said, "You can go to the bathroom now Sandra."

I nodded and pushed. They scooted me to the end of the bed. Her head was rather stuck. The doctor told me that he could help her a little. He had to use forceps around her head to pull her out. I did not get any stitches. I went back to school in April. It was a little hectic taking care of my new baby and studying. Thank God for mom Bernice. It was even more hectic getting all of my grades transferred to Edmondson Senior High School. Mom Bernice and I finally completed it all. Graduation was going to be in May. I was so happy. I finally made it. Joseph and I, even went to the prom, we were looking so good. Portia hooked up my makeup. We double dated with a girlfriend whom I met in school. We had a lot in common. Her name was Gwendolyn and she had two sons. Teenage girls were getting pregnant in other places besides York, Pennsylvania. I wish I could have told those white nurses I overheard talking about the black pregnant teens in York, Pennsylvania back in nineteen hundred and sixty five.

Chapter 18

Graduation at the Baltimore Civic Center

I MAILED ALL OF MY INVITATIONS out to my mom, Mr. Bill and my siblings. I would be the first one of my mother's children to graduate from high school. I was so full of joy. This was the first step in getting my life in order. I had promised mom and myself a long time ago that I was going to complete high school no matter how long it took. None of them knew I had given birth to a new baby girl, Karmentrina. I never told mom because she may have had a heart attack on the spot. My plan was to go back to York with my family and they would see her at the same time.

Saturday morning arrived, and it's graduation day. The streets are already full of cars and kids playing. Graduation ceremony scheduled for 6 pm. A car pulls up, and it was mom, Mr. Bill, and my youngest sister, Bonita. Mom came in the house first and saw the baby in the bassinet. She asked me whose baby it was. I told her I was babysitting for a friend. Portia looked at me and smiled.

Mom Bernice was sitting in the kitchen drinking a shot glass of Cutty Sark Scotch. Mom asked her who I was babysitting for and mom Bernice said, "She is babysitting for herself."

Mom put her hand to her head and sat down in the kitchen chair. She said, "Oh, Lord," and poured herself a shot glass of scotch. Scotch was not my mom's drink.

Bonita came into the house, and I told her it was my baby; I still have the pics of her with Karmentrina. Bonita picked her up from the bassinet. She would not let anyone else hold her. We took two cars to the graduation. Mom Bernice watched all of my three children so my family and Portia could attend the graduation ceremony with me. Joseph met us there.

There were over twelve hundred students graduating that evening. A person called your name and you stood up out of your chair and sat back down. We already had our fake diplomas in our hands. We would get our official diplomas in the mail later. We all left and went back to Mom Bernice's house, played records, danced and ate fried chicken, potato salad, and greens that Mom Bernice prepared earlier that day.

I ended up not going to York that night because there was not enough room for the kids and me. Mom came back for all of us a few weeks later, and we took all of my belongings. I moved in with my Mom at 471 ½ West College Avenue, York, Pennsylvania. That would be a pivotal place in my life. Joseph would come three weeks later and move in with us.

I went to see all of my other sisters to catch up on the York Gossip Line. I found out that Mary was still in that abusive relationship and now it was worse because she married Clabber Richardson. I told her to remember what mom went through for years with William. You cannot protect your children if you cannot protect yourself. I do not want to see you in a casket because he killed you. I told her that she needed to get her head on straight, buy a gun, and protect herself. Mary had tears in her eyes and was shaking her head yes, in agreement with me. She did purchase a gun and later freed herself from him. I knew she had it in her and just needed to find her inner strength to survive that horrible, abusive relationship.

Chapter 19

Widowed At Age 19

ON JUNE 25, NINETEEN HUNDRED and sixty eight, early in the evening, someone knocked at the front door. Joseph answered the door. He had just come home from work. Mabel, Mr. Bill, and I were in the kitchen cooking. My kids were sitting in front of the television. Mabel called me because she heard Joseph arguing with a man out front. I ran to the door. When I stepped out into the vestibule, a man was holding a gun on Joseph. The man was on the bottom step of four or five. I did not know who he was. He was asking Joseph to come out and get into his car.

Joseph said, "I am not going to come down and get into your car."

The man said, "Let's go now, Joe."

Joseph said, "No man, I am not going."

He accused Joseph of giving his wife gonorrhea. Joseph tried to explain that he did not know his wife. Joseph had only been back in York for three weeks. By this time, I am begging him not to shoot Joseph. The man walked up the steps and started shooting. I begged him to stop and he kept coming. He shot six times and shot Joseph directly with a 22-caliber handgun. Three of the bullets hit Joseph. The first bullet hit him in the lower chest; he grabbed his chest and started falling backwards to his left side. The second bullet hit Joseph in his back on the right side. The third bullet hit him in his left temporal brain. The perpetrator ran to his car and drove off. I kneeled down, leaned over Joseph, and started shaking him and yelling please do not die. Blood was all over me when the police arrived; they thought I was shot as well. Kimmy Jo and Kevin ran outside to the vestibule where I was. Karmentrina was in the crib. Someone called the police. Neighbors and people just passing by the area surrounded our apartment. Kevin was walking over to his dad and telling people, "My dad's nose is bleeding."

My friend Frankie came from around on Green Street (we were very close.) She took my kids to her house. The ambulance showed up as well as the police, several cars. They took Joseph away in the ambulance. I went with him. Someone contacted my mom who worked across the street at Dentist Supply, a factory. Mom and Mr. Bill came to the emergency room at the York Hospital and found me. Mr. Bill was in the apartment during the whole episode. However, he was not outside on the porch. The police were still asking me questions. So many, I could hardly think straight. I told them that the gunman accused Joseph of giving his wife a venereal disease. Mom looked very sad, as did Mr. Bill. Joseph was taken to the radiology department and then to the Intensive Care Unit. Mom, Mr. Bill, and I soon left to go home.

We found out from neighbors that evening that the perpetrator's name was Butchie Jamison, the brother of my friend, Freddie Jamison. Joseph died about 7 am the next morning (6/26/1968) in the intensive care unit at York Hospital. I found that out through a phone call when

I phoned the hospital to see how he was doing, and the nurse told me Joseph had expired. At that time, I did not know what that meant. My mom was standing beside me. I gave her the phone. When she hung up, she told me that Joseph had died. Since Joseph lived overnight, the charge was not first-degree murder, but murder and first-degree manslaughter. The autopsy report stated that Joseph was shot at 11 pm in the evening 6/25/1968, eleven days after my nineteenth birthday. I am positive about that time because Joseph had just arrived home from work. (There is more to that story and if you ever meet me and ask me about it, I may tell you). Joseph usually got home about 4 to 5 pm, so that 11 pm notation was simply not true. It was definitely early evening. Black on Black crime met nothing then. It does not mean that much now.

I was now a nineteen-year-old widow with three kids. Not too many people witness a murder. Then return to that same home and be reminded daily about the death of the person who was shot there and later died. Not just any person died there, but your husband and the father of your children. I am so sorry. Even though it was years ago, some memories never, fade. I cried day in and day out; I could not get it together. He died the same way his mother died, gun violence. Remembering how hurt he was when he lost his mother. I was so mad at God and thinking why would he let this happen. It was like asking God why he let William beat Dot when I was a little girl. I just could not focus on anything. I had to go to court and my mom went with me. I do not remember very much from that day. I remember being on the stand, and I was asked maybe one or two questions. I have no recollection of what the questions were. His family got the best attorneys, and he did no prison time for that murder. I believe the charge was not guilty. I think he served a year or so for some type of mental health care. I do not know if that was outpatient or in-patient. I just knew it felt wrong.

It was Fourteen months after John Jamison murdered my husband when he was out of the York County Jail. *(Article from the York Pennsylvania Local Newspaper) "Freed on Sanity Data – Yorker acquitted in Slaying; Released from jail after psychiatric report. A twenty-year-old York man, John A. Jamison, Junior, 41 East College Avenue was acquitted on 21 August 1969 of murder and manslaughter by reason of insanity in the June 26ᵗʰ shooting of Joseph Kearse, twenty-one at his home at 471 ½ West College Avenue was released by Presiding Judge George W. Atkins from the York County Jail, where he had been lodged since the slaying in June 1968. Judge Atkins acted on the findings of two Harrisburg Psychiatrist that he had appointed in November 21, 1968 to examine Jamison as petitioned on September 9, 1968 by the District Attorney under the State Mental Health Act. Doctor Warren J. Muhlfelder and Miles D. Garber Junior found him no longer suffering from mental illness and not in need of further confinement.*

At a brief hearing following receipt today of the report from Dr. Garber, who saw no merit in having Jamison followed by a local psychiatrist, or clinic. Judge Atkins adopted the recommendation in the January 20, 1969 report by Doctor Warren J. Muhlfelder that he report at regular intervals to the York Mental Health Center for an observation period of one year in order that the clinic may have an opportunity to check his mental health and institute appropriate measures should they become necessary.

No Objections *– Assistant District Attorney Earl R. Doll advocated this course in view of the seriousness of the crime and the lack of knowledge as to how Jamison may react in the community again, and Defense Council Richard Noll said Jamison had no objections when he discussed the recommendation with him two days ago. Noll added that he and co-counsel Attorney Richard E. Bergdoll fully concurred with the report and accepted them on their face value. Judge Atkins directed Jamison to get an appointment with The County Mental Health Center, to keep faithfully all appointments, and to undergo any treatments prescribed by the staff until they determine no further treatment is required. Judge*

Atkins directed the center to report to the court at six-month intervals, and more frequently if necessary, and ask council to cooperate with the center by supplying background information. The psychiatrist reports were turned over to the clerk of courts Clair R. Stine to become part of the record of the case.

Before the court case started, the court appointed defense attorneys told me that John Jamison said his wife told him that she had sex with Joseph and he infected her with venereal disease, which he contracted from her. An autopsy performed on Joseph one day after his death reported that Joseph did not have a venereal disease. Joseph had only been back in York Pennsylvania for about three weeks. Hardly enough time to form a relationship with anyone. Joseph lost his life based on a lie. May his wife forever bare that cross.

I was so hurt and felt abandoned by Joseph, even though it was not his fault. The perpetrator's brother came to see me a few weeks later and told me that his mother, Mrs. Jamison, wanted to see me, and I asked him why. He said she was so sorry and wanted to see me in person to tell me that. I felt some kind of way, but I did go to see her because Freddie was my friend.

Meeting and seeing her was very painful for I could see that she felt as bad as I did; she was so visibly hurt to me. She hugged me and her motherly touch made me feel a kind of peace. I told her she did not have to apologize and that I would be okay. That helped me to move on and I hoped that it helped her also.

We had a lot to do after Joseph's death; mostly mom took care of everything. I was walking around in a daze. Luckily for me, Joseph and I had life insurance policies that mom encouraged me to get when I moved to York with her. I remember the insurance man used to come every two weeks on Friday to collect two dollars and fifty cents on each policy. Mom called the insurance man and told him about Joseph's death. When Joseph died, the insurance policy was behind one week. The insurance man knew mom for years told her that he would put the money in for us and he backdated the payment. Mom had insurance policies with him for many years on herself and all of her children. She took me off the policy when Joseph and I started our own family insurance policy. Mom and I made the funeral plans. I remember taking my children to view their father's body at the Funeral home. It would be the last time they would ever see him. Kimmy 3, Kevin 2, and Karmentrina were 3 months old. I was carrying Karmentrina and Kimmy Jo and Kevin were by my side.

Mary was with us. Kimmy and Kevin at their young ages knew something was wrong, and they started asking me questions. "Why is daddy sleeping in that box? Is he going to stay here now?"

I told them that daddy was sleeping because he was tired from work and that God wanted him to live with him so he will not ever get tired again. I touched him and said goodbye along with the kids. This was so not real to me. Kimmy wanted to know how he was going to go with God. Mary chimed in and said that when we leave, he will come and get him.

The children did not go to the funeral. It was on 6/29/1968. Joseph buried at Lebanon Cemetery. After the funeral, for days, my neighbor Deborah Wright (Deb) who lived next door with her mom Miss Sissy and her three brothers, Leon (Smickel), Mike and Darryl (Boo) Wright would sit on our stoop and talk for hours on end. Sometimes my friend Frankie Chambers would come from around the corner, from Green Street, to sit, and talk with us. Nineteen hundred and sixty-nine was a hot turmoil summer.

I cannot remember anything about the funeral service today. It just disappeared from my mind. I often think about being hypnotized to remember what happened. It is gone. I feel today that the tragedy was most harmful, mentally to Kimmy Jo and Kevin Scott. They were ages two and three. Karmentrina was only three months old. No one was pushing for therapy for post-traumatic stress during those days. No one was doing civil suits either, because today, it would be a wrongful death civil suit. Kevin Scott had a slow start at birth. He had trouble in Head Start and kindergarten. They recommended testing at the York Hospital to see where he was at mentally. A mental health therapist told me that Kevin was borderline retarded.

I cried all the way home from the York Hospital to my mom's house on West College Avenue. My mom told me in her exact words, "That child ain't in no damn way retarded; don't believe them doctors at that damn hospital."

A child psychologist in Washington, District of Columbia tested Kevin later. Dr. Barbara Suter rendered a battery of tests to Kevin. She informed me that the test given to Kevin Scott at the York Hospital was an incorrect diagnosis. Dr. Barbara Sutter told me that the York Hospital Therapist rendered only one test to Kevin, which was very subjective.

Soon my mom moved around the corner on Green Street and left Mabel and me in the apartment. I could not deal with the memory, so I moved around the corner with my Mom. Soon my mom moved again to South Penn Street and left me in the small house. I guess she had enough of babies being around her. It was cool; I knew everyone on that short street. My Uncle James lived a few houses up from me. I became good friends with his girlfriend's daughter, Rita. We hung for a while. My bestie Frankie Chambers lived across the street. Frankie Chambers and Yvette Palmer who liked my cousin Douglas Smallwood used to sit out on the porch and talk with me. A boy lived across the Street named Rodney E. Brown. He and I became acquainted quickly. I was careless at that time and hated the world. I became pregnant with his child. Gossip had the word on the street about my pregnancy. Two of his female first cousins told Rodney to deny the pregnancy. Mary was friends with one of the cousins and told her to tell me to blame the pregnancy on my late husband; no one would know the wiser. I needed to get the hell off Green Street.

Chapter 20

Welcome Keenan Wynn
South Penn Street

MARCH 25, 1969, I WENT into labor and phoned Bonita who, at that time, was living with our dad, William. I was home alone with my three children. Bonita showed up in a taxicab, and I hopped into the same cab she exited. I was more than ready to get through this childbirth. March 25, 1969, Keenan Wynn Kearse, my new baby boy, was born. He was five months younger than Mabel's baby Clifford (Bubbles) was. He was beautiful, dark curly hair dark round eyes, looking like his father who did not want him. His aunt Avis Brown (Rest In peace) always stuck by me and loved my son. Later in life, Avis introduced Keenan, to many of his cousins who did accept him.

I had signed papers prior to this birth for a tubal ligation, yes, and no more children from this baby oven. All was going well at home with my children by now. Kimmy Jo was now 4 years of age, Kevin Scott 3 years of age, Karmentrina was now 1 year old, and my niece Tracey was 7 years of age and back living with her Mom, Mary again. She lived with me off and on. I enrolled Kimmy Jo and Kevin Scott in the local Head Start Program, and they were accepted. That gave me a break during the day, just taking care of Karmentrina and the new baby. Additionally, I babysat my nephew Bubbles during the night for my mom who now had him. Mom was working on the night shift.

One afternoon before Bubbles was with my mom, when Keenan was about six weeks old, beginning of May 1969, I walked across the street to my mom's house with Keenan and Karmentrina to see what she was doing. When I got there, she was happy to see the kids and me. We talked for a few minutes when she asked me if I had seen Mabel. I told her not lately but if you watch the kids for a few minutes, I will walk to her house to see if she is ok. Mom said, "Okay, Sandra, do not stay all day. I have to work tonight, and I have not slept yet."

I walked the few blocks from South Penn Street to West College Avenue. On my arrival, I knocked on the door and she did not answer. I knocked harder and then started pounding on the door. I was worried that Mabel may have been hurt in the apartment. She always had heart issues; she could have had a heart attack or something. I was thinking all kinds of stuff. I had to get into the apartment. My little nephew, Larry, was now looking out of the front window, and I could hear the baby, Bubbles, crying. Larry was not big enough at one year old or so to open the front door. Therefore, I climbed over a short brick wall on the side of the porch. I noticed the window not locked. I opened the window and climbed in. I picked up Larry, hugged and kissed him, put him down, and went to look for Bubbles. Bubble was in the crib with little or no movement. He was about five months old then I wrapped him in a blanket that he was lying on and then I dressed Larry, and I took my two nephews to my mom's house. When she saw the kids, she started cussing and crying at the same time.

Mabel showed up about a day later looking for her kids and of course, she knew I took them because neighbors always talked.

Mabel presented herself in a fit asking where her kids were, and I told her mom had them. Mabel was always the best curser out of all of us. She started cussing me out, slammed my front door, and left to go to mom's house. I telephoned mom to let her know Mabel was coming. Mom answered the phone and said she wanted her ass to come. She was waiting for her. Mom would not give Bubbles back to her but did return Larry. Mabel was mad at me for a few weeks but then she calmed down, and we were okay again. We were all too young to be moms. Mabel told us that she had left her boys with a girlfriend of hers and that she was the one who left them in the house alone.

I had a new boyfriend, Leon (Smickel) Wright. He was very good and protective to my children and me. He was not a stranger to me and knew what I had gone through in the past year. We used to live next door to each other. He was with me throughout my pregnancy with Keenan Wynn. He pretty much claimed my son, Keenan. Rodney Eugene Brown, Keenan's father, One day during the riots of July nineteen hundred and sixty nine, showed up on the scene. He was driving his big black Cadillac. He was blasting his music on the car radio and waving to everybody like he was a superstar. Leon and I were on the corner with many other people when he showed up. *Why did he have to show up now?*

Leon saw him, went over, and snatched him out of his car, calling him a no-good punk who could not take care of his child. Leon Smickel Wright roughed Rodney up quite a bit. I told Leon that was not necessary because I did not want anything from Rodney or any of his family. In a way I was damn glad he whipped his ass. I was most likely praying for it. That was something I should have not been praying to happen to him. He denied my son and got what he deserved that evening.

Sometime after the birth of Keenan, I noticed that my baby could not turn his head side-to-side in a half turn. When I took him to his well-baby visits at the Princess Street Clinic, the doctor said it was no big deal. I tried not to pay too much attention to it, but I did keep a close eye on him.

One day, several weeks after Keenan's birth, I was home alone and started to have some vaginal bleeding. At first, just a little bit and then quickly flowing likes a water faucet. I had no choice but to send Kimmy Jo (age four then) to her Aunt Mary's house about one block away on Penn Street. I had sent my niece Esther, who was Joseph's youngest sister, to the store with a note for pads she brought them back to me. Kimmy Jo had to cross two streets. I wrote a note for Mary to come and she did. I watched out of the front door as Kimmy Jo ran to take the note to Mary. Mary came a running and I called the police who arrived in about ten minutes and took us to the York Hospital emergency room. I was worried about my kids; I left my kids alone with their Aunt Esther who was only about ten years-old or so. Leon was not home; he was at the park playing basketball at the time. There were no cell phones or pagers back then, so I could not contact him.

We arrived at the emergency room and they needed to do some kind of surgical procedure. They were talking to Mary and she was agreeing with them, as if she was my mom. I had to let them know she was not my mom. The doctor said there was no time to wait and I was old enough, and along with my sister, we needed to make a decision. The situation was dire, so I agreed. I had to have my uterus packed with so much packing to stop the bleeding. It felt like I was five months pregnant. The packing had to stay in place for five days and then back to the hospital to have the packing removed. On my arrival, back home after the hospital episode, Leon was home. When I went back to the hospital to have the packing removed, my mom was with me. The doctor told mom and me that I had uterine cancer. The report came from the biopsy they did when they put the packing in. I ask the doctor if I was going to die and he said not if he could help it. I had some procedures and treatment and the cancer did not return. This was one of many blessings for me from God.

When Keenan was about four months old, I started to work at the York Hospital Emergency Room as a unit secretary. I worked many evening shifts. I did not have a car nor did Leon, but he had a friend who would pick me up after work and give me a ride home sometimes. This one particular evening, Leon asked his friend, Sam P, to give me a ride home. Sam P. decided he would take the scenic route. I asked him where he was going since this was not the way to my house. He said we could go this way. I knew my way to the reservoir in York, Pennsylvania close to the York Hospital. Now I was quiet and kept my mouth shut, but I was thinking, *Sam P, if you do something to me you better kill me because Leon is surely going to kill you.* He drives on the back road and pulls over, turns off the car and slides over to my side of the front seat.

I asked, "Is it your plan to rape me? Go ahead; I am not even going to resist you. Get it over with Sam."

He must have thought about it and decided to apologize and drive me home. He kept repeating himself, "I am sorry Lou, please just say something."

I was saying a lot to myself and if it came out of my mouth, he may not have taken me home. Leon was home when I got there. He already picked up the kids from my mom's house.

He asked, "What took you so long? Did Sam pick you up?"

I answered back, "Yes, he did, but he took the scenic route." Leon was holding Karmentrina on his lap. The rest of the kids were sleeping.

He said, "What the fuck do you mean?"

I said, "I think he was planning to have sex with me."

Leon tensely asked, "Did he fucking touch you?"

I said, "He tried to put his hand under my dress. I gave him a look and he stopped and brought me home."

Leon was livid asking if anything else happened, and I told him no. Next thing I know, he is giving me Karmentrina to me to hold. He was prancing and biting his hand as he did when he was angry. He soon calmed down. Everything eventually seemed cooled down, and we went to bed with Karmentrina and Keenan between us. That was the norm for my two babies.

The next day the rumors were flying. Mary called and asked if I heard what Leon did to Sam P. I asked what he did. Apparently, he went to his job, snatched him off the trash truck, and beat him with a trashcan. They said a few people had to pull Leon off Sam P. I was laughing on the phone and Mary asked what happened. I told her about my episode with Sam P., and she agreed that he deserved it. He will think about it the next time he tries to touch something that does not belong to him.

I soon joined a local singing group. That was fun because I enjoyed singing and I wanted to get back to singing again. I was always in somebody's singing group. My plate was full with four children and a niece, working, and performing with a singing group. That kept me occupied for about two years. On July 12, 1969 my paternal grandmother, Mabel Paul Smallwood passed. There are so many stories I remember from when my siblings and me stayed overnight at her house. Aunt Sis and Uncle James lived on either side of Grandmom Mabel. Grandpop Buddy use to scare us when we went to bed. He would make noises as if someone was on the stairs. He would say in a low voice, "Red Eyed Bloody Bones is on the first step coming to get you." All of us would be screaming for Grandma Mabel. She would yell at Grandpop and tell him to stop scaring us – because we needed to go to sleep. Grandma moved to 432 West Hope Avenue when I was older. I used to walk around the corner from Penn Street to see what she was doing. One day I peeped into her front room window and she was listening to the radio to Chubby Checker and doing the twist. I called out to her through the window, "Hey grandma, I caught you doing the twist."

Grandma responded back, "Child don't you go telling anybody that." I laughed with her and went inside to see what goodies she had. I had my kids with me they knew Grandmom kept cookies in her cookie jar.

She died soon after that. I attended her funeral, and it was so crowded with relatives and grands, there were so many of us. Grandma's brothers came from Orangeburg, South Carolina and many other southern relatives. Both of grandma's brothers and their wives were present. They both married women with the name of Irene. Dottie Mae, Pokey, and I spent a six-week summer vacation with grandma Mabel's Brother Uncle Willie Paul and his wife, Aunt Irene. My son Keenan was about four months old at the time. Aunt Irene asked to hold Keenan. She noticed that when she called out to him, he did not turn his head completely towards her. Aunt Irene asked me why the baby bent his head that way. I told her the doctors at the well-baby clinic said it was no problem.

She said, "I swear there is no such thing! Child, let me tell you something; the white doctors go to those fancy schools and swear they have all the answers. You cannot believe everything they say. Baby cannot turn his head completely. That is Hogwash."

I told her what the well-baby clinic doctor said from the Princess Street Center. She told me to give the baby to my mom to hold. I did. She took a small clear bottle from her pocketbook. I asked her what was in it and she said it was her Holy Water. God had blessed the water. I was thinking just how she got that water from God. I did not care as long as it worked.

Aunt Irene started to rub the holy water all over Keenan's neck. She told me to stand behind my mom first on her right side and then on her left side and call Keenan. I did and Keenan turned completely around followed my voice and looked for me. I was like, "Mom, Keenan turned his head to both sides." Mom said if she had not witnessed it, she would not have believed this miracle. Mom looked over at Uncle James and said, "James fix me a drink."

Darn right, I believe in the Holy Spirit. I always did since I was a small child; I knew something or someone was in my corner. I do not think it was about the Holy water. I believe now that it was my aunt's bond with God. That is why the miracle happened. I truly believe that one must have a bond with God to have a decent and protected life.

Chapter 21

The Death of Martin Luther King, Junior

I N 1968-1969, THERE WAS A war on in York. Those two summers were volatile times for us living in York Pennsylvania. The 1969 race riots occurred. Apparently, a black youth burned his self-playing with lighter fluid. He blamed it on a local white gang known as the Girarders. That later would be revealed as a lie, but not before the pent-up resentments of the black community turned violent. (Documented York Local Newspaper) It was a period of racial unrest. Racially polarizing murders and investigations by the police was going on. The 1,117 state Law enforcement agencies employed 27,413 sworn police officers to end the riots in Pennsylvania. An early afternoon curfew mandated that people be kept off the streets. Our young people were breaking into stores, burning building and preparing for the worse with guns of their own. The riots were happening everywhere. Martin Luther King's assassination on April 4, 1968 brought about out of -control race riots in Washington, DC, and in addition, 110 U.S. other cities. York did not want to deal with the same unrest. I did not come out of my house after the 3 pm curfew time. There was a stop to everything pretty much. You could hear gunfire all day and all night long and no one would venture outside unless necessary. I did not bring my kids out of the house unless I was walking to my mom's house. I sometimes went with Leon to his mom's around the corner. The kids would be with us.

One evening after curfew, Leon and I were out and missed curfew. We heard a truck coming over the College Avenue Bridge and we hid between a parked car and the street curb. We watched the big armored National Guard truck ride by, policing our street, and we stayed there on the ground until the armored truck was gone.

I decided York was not for me any longer. Young mothers like myself, sitting out on our porches all day or sitting in the park all day talking about life but not living our lives as we wanted to or desired to. I was not only struggling with my four children; I was trying to hold on to Esther who ran away from her aunt to live with me. She said her aunt was beating her and her siblings all the time. Esther was only ten years old and I could see the hurt in her eyes. I took her to her aunt's house to get some of her clothing and her aunt told me, "She won't get any damn clothes from here."

I looked her in her face and said I would buy her some new clothes. I had a little money from my widow's pension. Esther thought I was so tough (Smile). If Esther only knew, I was scared as hell of her aunt. Her mom was dead; her brother Joseph was dead, her eldest sister Jeanette was dead and died three months after Joseph died. She died of liver disease. Esther lived with me for a little while, but I knew I was too young to be a mother to her. I did not know how to be a mom to my own children. Mom helped me out with getting Esther a home where she would be safe; we did that. I always kept in touch and had her come to my house for visits as much as I could. She was a very sweet and vulnerable little girl. We still have a strong bond today.

Life still seemed unpredictable to me. I just could not get both of my feet planted in a stable place. I was ready to get away from York. So ready for a new, start without Leon. It was time to lean on my mom again. She was my rock. I talked with my mom about how I was feeling, and she said she would talk to my cousin, Tiny, who lived in Philadelphia, Pennsylvania (Philly) to see if I could move to Philly and stay with her for a while. (Tiny was mom's niece, who lived with us from time to time on Codorus Street). When I left York, Pennsylvania and moved to Philadelphia, Pennsylvania Leon was heartbroken. It was time for me to make a change and I did. I had to find myself.

When I moved to Philadelphia, I went alone, and my mom took care of my children. The first thing on my agenda was to learn the metro and bus system and put in multiple applications to find a job. I finally found a job at Saint Christopher's Children's Hospital as a unit secretary. While staying with my cousin Tiny, my Mom sent her rent money for me, along with a few dollars for my incidentals. I had my social security check sent to my mom's house because she had my kids. I started paying my cousin out of my paycheck when I was working so I told my Mom to stop sending her money. Tiny was a little upset about that and said she needed more money from me. In my mind, I did not want to give her any more of my damn money, but I did because I was homeless. If she could have only read my mind, she would have kicked me out. Tiny had a beauty shop in her basement and sometimes I would help her out around the shop. One day a woman named Patti Jean came into the shop to get her hair done. Apparently, she was a regular client. I was in the shop just sitting. While she was under the dryer, Tiny had gone upstairs for a while; she lifted up the hood and started talking to me.

She said, "You don't look happy." In addition, I said, "I am not." I felt comfortable sharing with her what I was going through living with my cousin Tiny. Patti Jean surprised me and invited me to live with her and her little girl. It was about two blocks up the street from where I was. The Holy Spirit told me I could trust her, and I left the next day with my little suitcase. I left Tiny a short note, GOODBYE TINY. I did appreciate Tiny, I absolutely did, but when she no longer controlled my money, she changed. Tiny had helped me to find a house to buy from someone she and her husband knew prior to me leaving her house. I had the connections to the realtor. So living with her and Patti Jean was a temporary situation.

I worked and saved money just waiting for my house to come through. Patti lived alone with her daughter. I told her all about my kids and she said I could bring them to Philly if I wanted to. I chose to bring Kimmy Jo because she was the same age of Patti's little girl. Patti watched Kimmy Jo while I worked and later, she kept the rest of my children when they came to be with me. Patti and I never exchanged money and sometimes I watched her little girl when she had things to do. Patti thought I was bored just working and being home with the kids. She decided that I needed to meet some friends. She introduced me to her man friend who introduced me to one of his friends, J. We double dated from time to time. Her babysitter would watch the kids. Patti introduced me to the world, as she knew it. I learned how to play the street numbers (illegal back then). One day I put $0.25 cents on a number and won $40.00. A good return for twenty five cents. Patti introduced me to the gypsy world of fortunetellers. I was cool with it until one of the readers told me to bring her six eggs, two carrots, and one onion. I did bring her the items, but I was not feeling it. I knew I could not afford to feed the gypsies and my family too. I do not go to fortunetellers today.

Not long after meeting J, I was going out alone with him. We went to closed card parties. We went out clubbing, even though I was not twenty-one years of age yet. I noticed that everyone catered to him. J. introduced me as his girl. I never knew we were a couple. One evening when I got home from work, he called me and told me to take a taxicab to Center City in Philadelphia to meet him at a hotel where he was staying. I told him that I did not know where Center City was, and I could not waste my money on cabs to come and see him. He told me to get dressed and he would arrange for the cab and pay for it when I got there. I reluctantly agreed, and went immediately to Patti's room, and told her what he said.

She looked at me and said, "Guess you had better get dressed then." I told her I did not have any money, what if he is not there. Patti went into her bedside table, gave me a $20.00 bill, and said that should be enough. I wondered how I would get back if he were not there. She assured me she had my back and to trust her.

The taxicab showed up and asked for me by name. While riding to Center City, I was watching the meter with my heart beating rapidly as the meter creeped up to $19.00, I asked the driver how much further, and he said about 15 more blocks. I said to myself, *Lord let this Black man be there.* We arrived there and the meter read $22.00. He was standing outside sporting a red silk robe with a white collar, as if I was meeting Super Fly. He came over to the taxicab, paid the fare, and gave him a healthy tip. In the lobby, I used the pay phone to call Patti Jean and let her know I made it to the hotel safely.

We walked through the lobby and the staff was addressing him saying, "Mr. J, do you need anything?"

Now I am wondering who in the hell is this man. I followed him to the elevator and entered. The elevator man pressed the button for the Penthouse. I have never been in a Penthouse, so I certainly wanted to see it. The door opened up into an expansive, beautiful suite. I walked over to the large window to look out over the city. It was breathtaking. I was thinking, *ha-ha wish my sisters could see me now.* Everything you could think of was in that Penthouse. Jazz music was playing; incense was burning, marble floors with an awesome fire place lit. He was showing me around and told me we had the master suite. I asked did he have a roommate.

He said his boy and one of his hoes is here. I then asked him, "Am I your hoe?"

He said, "Not at all Saundra; I can get a hoe in the street any day and time. I do not bring hoes to my Penthouse."

He offered me a drink of red wine and said let us take it to my room. I said I could not do anything with other people in here, but he noted they were in a different room. I said that would not work for me. He said give me a minute and walked out of the room, went to the other bedroom, and told his friend he had to go. When he left the room, I was thinking, that might not have been a good move, now I would be alone. I started thinking about the *Perry Mason television episodes.* No, witness. I heard the elevator door open (ding ding), and they were gone. We got comfortable drinking wine and listening to jazz in the main bedroom suite. I took my coat, shoes off, and sat in the lounge chair, sipping on the wine. I was not a drinker and wanted to stay in control. This was the first time in my life that I was with a real man. *Not just, bit-bam, thank you ma'am.* We made real love. It opened up a completely new world for me of how a woman should be touched and how a woman should feel. If you do not know, you had better ask somebody! While I was relaxing and being touched by J. I was thinking he could send a taxicab for me anytime he wanted too. I would even miss work for episodes like this.

Riding home was calming; I did not even look out of the windows. I was so deep in thought. My body was in complete relaxation mode. When I arrived about five am in the morning, I woke Patti up and told her about my night of bliss. I told her I could not even explain the feelings I had experienced. Patti Jean laughed so much. She said, "Welcome to the city Saundra." I found out later that he was a hustler, not a pimp. I saw him off and on until my children came to live with me. I did not want that kind of man around my children. Patti Jean and I remained friends for a long time, and then we lost touch with each other when I left Philly.

Chapter 22

Hallelujah, Settlement Day Summer 1970

NOT TOO LONG AFTER LIVING with Patti Jean, I was able to purchase my own house. On settlement day, I woke us up very early in the morning and said, "Thank You God for this Gift. I will be forever grateful." I am the first one of my mother's children to buy a house. Settlement came through about eight weeks after I moved away from my cousin's house. This was a major accomplishment for me, along with my first accomplishment, which was graduating from high school.

My house was at 2033 Tulpehocken Street, in the Germantown area of Philadelphia. It was a single-family brick home. I remember walking up the concrete walkway to the steps to my large, front porch and feeling blessed beyond measure. I was like, "Wow, I bought this house and I didn't need a co-signer." Who would have thought a twenty-year old single mother with four children and one job could afford a new house? I remember sitting on the porch with Mother Walker back in York, PA. Mother Walker told me to open my own door and walk out because I was in my own self-trap. If I chose to not open doors, I would stay trapped. Mother Walker, see me now opening up these doors. The house had three bedrooms on the second floor and a full bath. The first floor had a living room, dining room, and a kitchen. The basement was large with a garage door entry. I thought I was in heaven. The house was empty, but there were curtains. My mom and Mr. Bill brought the rest of my kids to me, as well as some household items. I purchased a kitchen table with four chairs and a small black and white TV; we were in business. Keenan was still in a highchair. The house had carpeted flooring, so I did not initially worry about bedding. I had plenty of comforters and pillows that mom gave us to sleep on. My kids and I were quite happy.

When I left York, I gave all of my furniture away. I made enough money to purchase furniture. Every payday I purchased something we needed. The first was beds for my kids and then living room furniture, etc. I slept on the sofa. I remembered when we lived in Lancaster, Pennsylvania that Mom did not have a bedroom. She slept on our couch for about two years. It was no big deal to me. My kids and I would get on the train and ride to Reading, Pennsylvania to visit my sister-in-law, Cressie Kearse (rest in peace), and ride the train to York, Pennsylvania to visit my mom and siblings. Our first ride on the train was an amazing experience, for we had never been on a train before.

Soon it was time for Kimmy Jo to start kindergarten. I walked her to the school, which was about a half a block from where we lived. She cried and tried to hold on to me for dear life. Made me have a flashback to when I went to pre-kindergarten and did the same thing to my mom. The teacher told me to let her go, and so I walked away. After school Kimmy was supposed to wait for me on the corner, however, she did not; she walked away, and got lost a little. Some woman (thank God) saw her wandering about and returned her home. Kimmy Jo knew her address, which I taught all of them as soon as possible. This was a little scary for me. I looked high and low for her. It was only about twenty minutes or so, but it seemed like an eternity. I decided to be outside of her school to meet her from that point on.

Not quite settled in my new home when Mary, called me one day to ask if she could come to stay with me in Philadelphia for a while because she was experiencing some domestic violence bullshit with Clabber. I told her hell yes. She came with her three kids, Ching, Tara, and Jordan. Their ages mirrored my kid's ages somewhat. Her daughter, Tracey, was with mom and her son, Bernard, was with our dad, William. They stayed about two months or so. It helped me somewhat, as I did not need my local babysitter for now, and I could work swing shifts and make more money. Financially I was doing okay. My widow's pension and my paycheck were more than enough money for me to provide for us. I was working many evening shifts at St. Christopher's Children's Hospital. After work, I always tried to walk with another employee to the bus stop to transfer to the train because there had been several robberies and rapes in the area of the hospital.

This one particular night, I was a little late getting off work. I missed the 11:40 pm bus and had to get the next one at 12:15 am. My plan was to transfer to another bus to get home to avoid the subway train. When I arrived at my bus stop, I had to walk about a quarter of a block to transfer to the next bus. I was standing on the corner, waiting; it was dark and cold. I was quite nervous.

About five minutes into waiting for the next bus, a man came walking down the street with a hoodie on. The streetlight was out on the corner. The man started walking towards me, and I was so afraid. I just knew it was over for me. He walked so close to me, looked me in my face, and said, "Miss you got the time?" My hand was shaking so badly, that I could hardly lift my coat sleeve to tell him the time. Then he said, "What are you doing out here this late by yourself?" I explained to him about my transportation situation.

He said, "You should take the train; it would be quicker than the bus. Where are you going?" I told him. He said, "I am going that way; come on, I'll ride the train with you."

He rode the train all the way to my stop and started to walk me to my door. Now I was thinking to myself, *did I make a mistake?* He walked me to my door and said good night. Upon entry to my house, my four-year-old son Kevin was up waiting for me. He always did that. He wanted to sleep with me on the couch. I tucked him in and made myself a cup of hot chocolate, sat down to my table and said, "Thank you Jesus." Mary asked me what happened, and I told her the whole story.

I remember back when my siblings and me used to stay with Grandma Mabel back on West Gas Alley (they now call it Gas Avenue and the house still stands). She said, "You never know how Jesus will present himself to you. Therefore, if a stranger knocks on your door for a glass of cold water, you had better give him a big glass of cold water, because it might be Jesus." I felt it was Jesus that night. I never missed my bus again.

Just when I was quite comfortable with Mary and her kids, she decided she wanted to go back to York, Pennsylvania with her abusive husband. She arranged for someone to come and pick her up, and they came for her. We said our goodbyes and they were off to York. I now had to go back to my old babysitter's mother to see if her daughter could return to babysitting for me. It would keep me on the evening shift because she went to school during the day. I knew I wanted to work primarily day shift and was trying to figure out what I could do. I knew Bonita lived with my dad in York and that she had a little boy, Sean. I called my mom and asked her to convince Bonita to come and live with me. Bonita called me about two days after I spoke with mom, and she agreed. She was so happy, for she had never been to Philadelphia before. Mom and Mr. Bill drove her to Philadelphia along with her son, Sean. Babysitting problem now solved. What I did not know was that my baby sister was pregnant with a second child.

A few weeks after Bonita came to live with me, she told me that she thought she saw a man peeping through the front window while I was at work. I asked her who would do that in the daytime. She did not know, but she said she saw him. We went throughout the house and checked to see that all windows locked from the inside of the house. We also made sure that no one could enter through the basement garage door. We installed a lock on the kitchen door that lead to the basement garage. We were both a little scared about the thought of a Peeping Tom. Why did he choose our window to peep through? We started to keep the front porch light and the garage light on during the night. The garage light was behind the house, which is how one would enter through the basement. After a while, Bonita said she had not seen the Peeping Tom. I thought he was probably not feeling the lights being on.

Things were going good. I was learning all the secretarial skills I needed to move on to a better secretarial job until I had an incident with a resident. I was instructing a patient's parent on filling out some paperwork. I was bending over the counter a little to read the form when a white resident came by me and pressed into me. I jerked back and said, "What the fuck are you doing?" That phrase came out of my mouth before my brain could stop it. Things got very quiet. One could hear a pin drop.

The white charge nurse raised her voice at me and said, "Miss Kearse, do you know who you are talking too?"

135

I responded, "I do not give a hell whom he is. I do not belong to him."

By now, there is an audience and the charge nurse asked me to leave and clock out. The resident chimed in and said, "No she does not have to leave."

He actually apologized and told her he would handle it. I did clock out. I went to the locker room to get my pocketbook. It seemed very light when I picked it up. I looked inside and saw that my wallet was missing. Now I was really pissed off. I had some change that I always threw in my purse. I scraped the bottom and scrounged up enough change to take the bus home. I was so irritated. My purse had about forty dollars cash and my driver's license, along with my social security card. Way back then everyone carried a social security card. I worked on getting my replacement cards and it was not that hard.

About a week later, I received a big package in the mail. It was my big wallet with all of my cards. Of course, the money was gone. I believe that whoever took it was really in need because they cared enough to mail my wallet back to me. They could have thrown the wallet away. The mail carrier said someone dropped it in a mailbox. It had to be an employee because it was in the employee locker room.

I called the switchboard the next day to talk with a friend who worked the switchboard and told her what happened. When I was on the evening shift, I would go to the booth and learn how to work the switchboard. I asked her to check to see if I still had a job. She had not heard anything. I went back to work two days later like nothing ever happened. The resident squared everything up for me. About a week later or so, Mark, the white resident stopped by my floor and asked me out to lunch. I said, "You are white and I am black. I think that is a problem." He bugged the hell out of me until finally I accepted his invitation and his apology. I felt so uncomfortable. Everyone was staring at us in the restaurant. Mark told me not to worry about people looking and talking.

Soon everyone in the hospital was talking about us. He started taking me around his friends, and I knew then he was getting quite serious about me. The white nurses who were after Mark S. had no chance; it was my court and I was in charge. I thought it was time for me to tell him I had children. I told him I had four children at home, and they were not white. I told him they were the most important persons in my life. He was cool.

I visited all of the sections of the hospital where I knew his rotations would be. When he was rotating through the emergency room, he let me mask and gown up and he taught me how to put in sutures in patients. He told me no one would know, just watch what I do and then you follow.

I met a white nurse who worked with him, named Patricia, and she was dating Sammy Davis, Jr. Back then. We became the best of friends. Finally, I told my mom about Mark.

Mom said, "Lord Jesus, child is you crazy?" I could almost feel her emotions running through me. Mom had some advice for me. "Sandra Lee, you cannot marry that white man. In this day and time, it will not work. How will you and your kids fit into his world?"

I had not given that too much thought. I told my mom that I was not thinking about marrying anybody. I did not particularly like playing wife when I was married for real to Joseph.

I was getting so close to Mark that it scared me. I started to think what if he wanted me to have a child for him. That was impossible for me. In addition, I did not want any more children. I called my self-breaking up with him with a new resident who showed up at the hospital. His name was Jeffrey from South Africa; he started making passes, and I played hard to get. Hospitals are like little Peyton Places, where everyone knows what is going on. Of course, Jeffrey heard about Mark and me. He asked me if we were a couple. To make a long story short, I started dating Jeffrey. He was cool. I told Patti Jean about him. She was excited and wanted to meet her own intern from the hospital. I invited her to go with me to a picnic and while there Jeffrey introduced her to an intern named Carlos from South America. They hit it off well and Patti started seeing him. The way he said Patti's name made her melt. She could not shut up about him. Jeffrey had an accent also, but not like Carlos. One day Patti and I attended a party. Jeffrey and Carlos invited us. Carlos was driving. We pulled up to a mansion and felt like we were in the wrong place.

When we walked in, there was a very large foyer with people everywhere. Jeffrey found a seat for us and he and Carlos decided to walk around and mingle. Hell, Patti and I did not know anyone at the party. We were sitting for a few minutes, and I decided we needed to mingle too. We headed over to the bar and a man, looking so good, offered us a glass of wine. We accepted. We started talking to people. We bumped into Jeffrey and Carlos about twenty minutes later.

Carlos said to Patti, "It looks like you and Sandra are having a good time."

She said, "Yes, we are."

Jeffrey looked at me and asked where the drinks came from. We looked at him like some kind of stupid. I told him from the bar. A nice man offered, and we accepted. Jeffrey went off on a tangent and said, "Sandra (in his African Accent) when you are with me, you do accept drinks from a strange man. I will get drinks for you."

Let us keep it real. I was grown widow with four children and a job. I may have been young, but I was adult enough to know I did not like his tone of voice. My mind was responding to him nonverbally. *Who in the hell was he talking to?* I dared not to say it aloud because I did not know where we were, and I was not driving. I knew we drove some distance to get there. That relationship was in a bad place from that point on. I woke up. I turned cold, and he tried harder to get back into my good graces. He wanted to marry me and take my children and me to Africa, where he said my children and me would live well because of his status. That was not a choice for me, trapped in a world that I did not belong in. I heard a man could have many wives in his country. I slowly pulled away from Jeffrey.

In the meantime, back at the house, Bonita was having problems with her pregnancy. She was not seeing a doctor in Philly. It was time for her to go back home to get care. She and Sean went back to York on the Greyhound Bus. The school year was ending for Kimmy Jo now. So when Bonita left, I felt lonely for her and York.

Like I usually did when I was feeling blue, I called my mom and told her that Philly life was too fast for me. I needed to come back to York and regroup. I thought maybe Rodney Brown's female cousins were done gossiping about me. The ones who said I should blame my baby on my late husband Joseph Kearse.

My mom said, "Sandra Lee do not pay them folks any mind. They are not taking care of you or your son."

I never asked for child support because I did not want to deal with him or his family. They thought they were high above my station. I asked my mom to see if Mr. Bill would come and move me back to York. He agreed and came for me with a friend to drive the U-Haul truck. I went to the realtor who sold me the house and asked him to rent it out for me. He did rent it out for me at good rental fee

We rented a U-Haul and left Philly, along with leaving my male suitors, Mark and Jeffrey. It just was not in the cards. We did not have cell phones then, so I was not worried about them tracking me down. Unfortunately, Bonita lost her baby whom she named Sandra, after me. I was honored and sad for her at the same time. My kids and me left Philadelphia soon after Bonita left.

We moved in with my mom on West College Avenue. Lugenia (Pokey) lived in a house next door to mom. She was planning to move with her boyfriend, Rock Mitchell, and soon left the house. Mom talked to the property owner who owned her house and Pokey's house to see if I could move into it. It all worked out and Bonita who was living on South Street with William and Mary asked if she could come and live with me again, and I told her of course. I always spoiled her and Bucky.

The house was a little further up from the house where the man shot Joseph on West College Avenue, across from Dentist Supply Company. We lived together for a while. Bonita and I also arranged for our kids to ride the Redline Bible Church Sunday school bus for Sunday school every week. I wanted to have organization in my life as soon as possible and prepare to move on to greater independency. I signed up for a subsidized housing project so I could have my own place without my sister. While I lived with my sister, we enjoyed each other's company

I remember when the food truck with all kinds of pastries and hot drinks would park across the street in front of The Dentist Supply Company for employees. Bonita and I would get big cinnamon rolls and hot chocolate to eat after I walked Kimmy Jo, Kevin, and Karmentrina to school. We had to walk for several blocks across the College Avenue Bridge, through Penn Park to Head Start first. Then back across the park to Saint Patrick's for Kimmy and Kevin's school. I remember when Bonita would get upset when my son Kevin would tell her at the dinner table that she had too much food on her plate. She would ask me to tell Kevin to stop saying that to her. I would laugh my ass off when she asked me. I did talk with Kevin about it. I told him it was not nice. Kevin reminded me that I told them to get a little bit on our plate to make sure they could eat it. I explained to him that grownups always get a lot more because they have big stomachs and they can eat it all.

Chapter 23

351 Stone Avenue York Pennsylvania

IT DID NOT TAKE VERY long for my name to come up on the project-housing list. I received a letter of acceptance near the end of the school year and we moved. I was so happy that I would now have bedrooms for my children. Hallelujah! Bonita and her boyfriend (whom she later married) Barry Banks took over the house when I moved out. Subsidized housing was another bubble created to keep poor people together, but it allowed me to be independent. My back door faced the street right in the back of the Penn Street houses. It was not like our house on Tulpehocken Street in Philadelphia a single-family brick house but it felt like it. We had a small fenced back yard, kitchen, large pantry, living room, three bedrooms, and a full bath and it was three blocks from my mom and one block from Mary and Mabel. My brother Bucky and our play brother Wayne Wilson practically lived at my house when I moved in. Pokey and Dottie Mae lived across the bridge on the east side of York with their husbands. The kids loved their new bedrooms and fell right into the new setting. In the backyard, I put up clotheslines to hang up clothing. I would walk to the laundry mat about four blocks away to wash laundry and use my cart to bring the wet laundry back to hang up in the yard. It was too costly to dry them at the laundry mat. They loved playing back there. Karmentrina and Keenan Wynn were playing on the backyard steps one afternoon. They got into a little spat and Keenan Wynn bit Karmentrina in the chest. She still bares that scar from her little brother. I ran outside and Karmentrina was screaming. Mom just happened to be there, and she came outside. I grabbed Keenan, shook him a little, and told him I was going to teach him about how that felt. I took his little skinny arm and went to bite him and mom would not let me bite him. Mom took Keenan in the house, put him across her lap, and gave him a spanking. Keenan sat on the floor crying his little heart out, tears and snot running down his little face. He was about two and Karmentrina was three.

I went to pick him up and mom said, "Leave him be Sandra Lee. He will be okay. He cannot go around biting people. You have to break him out of that right now."

I said to myself, as I do a lot, I was trying to teach him by letting him experience how it felt. Keenan stopped crying soon. His eyes were all red. Face all sad. He stood up, walked over to my mom, and put his head on her lap. She started rubbing his back and said to Keenan, "You okay now, you cannot go around biting people, okay?"

My Keenan turned his head and sunk his teeth into his grandma's thigh. Mom snatched him up and screamed, "Sandra Lee, that boy bit me!"

I snatched my baby from mom and told her, "Mom he is only two years old. You should have let me bite him when I wanted to outside in the yard. He didn't understand anything you did."

I pulled his little pant leg up and bit his thigh. I did not break his skin, but it was just enough pressure to give him a wakeup call. Keenan Wynn never bit anyone else.

I am into my routine and I was feeling comfortable in my skin for now. I ran into Leon. A relationship I did not want to rekindle. We remained friends forever. I played the single role for a while. Karmentrina was in kindergarten and Keenan was now in Head Start. I now had no children home during the day. I was not looking for a job right away. I wanted my feet to be on solid ground -- house straight, kids in school, etc. I put Kimmy, Kevin, and Karmentrina into the Catholic school system. Even though I was not Catholic, I felt they would get a better education. Kimmy Jo and a neighbor's son were in second grade together, Vincent Clayton. They were the only two black children in their first-grade class last year. One evening just before we sat down to dinner there was a knock on the door. I opened the door and a little boy with a folded paper in his hand was standing there.

He said, "Hello, my name is Vincent. My mom wanted me to give you this note."

I thanked him, and he ran back over to his house adjacent to our house. It was right next door to my kid's half-brother. It was a very short note. It said, "Hello my name is Joanne Clayton. My son and your daughter are the only two black children in their class at Saint Patrick's Elementary School. I think we should connect so we can support each other at that school." The note also read, "Come down to Freddie's Store on the corner of South Newberry and Princess Street tomorrow morning after the kids go to school to meet me."

The next morning after I walked Kimmy Jo, Kevin, and Karmentrina to school and Keenan to Head Start, I walked down to the store to meet Joanne Clayton. We became the best of friends from that day on. We connected instantly. We would become best friends until her passing September 28, 2012 (Joanne Clayton, Rest in Peace). I loved her unconditionally. We were always there for each other through thick and thin, good and bad times.

Time was flying and another year went by. My children were getting so big. One day when I went to meet Kimmy Jo, Kevin, and Karmentrina to walk home after we picked up Keenan, which was close by, Kimmy's hair was out of place. I had just braided her hair the night before and I would use a stocking cap at night to maintain her hair braids for 3 to 4 days. I asked Kimmy what happened to her hair and she said, "Miss Gentile grabbed my braids and shook my head because I didn't know the answer to my math problem. I was crying, mom, and I told Miss Gentile I was sorry."

In my head, I was saying to myself, *bitch you messed with the wrong Black little girl!* I told Kimmy Jo not to worry; I would braid her hair again. I told her I would have a talk with Miss Gentile the next day. I could hardly sleep that night. I was thinking about that white teacher who embarrassed my little girl. I do not know whose child she thought she was embarrassing in front of the entire classroom. What was she thinking?

The next day, I was so ready to approach that teacher. I decided to talk to my mom and get her take on it. She said, "That does not make any sense; you need to take Kimmy Jo and Kevin out of that white school."

I told my mom that Kimmy Jo and her siblings had every right to be in that school. I would not allow any person at that school to put their hands on my Kimmy Jo or any other child that I have because they deserve better. My children are going to see and know that I will protect them and fight for them whenever it is necessary.

I called Joanne, told her about it, and asked her what would she do? She said she would call for a conference with the teacher and Sister Mary Frances the Head Sister at the school. I heard her and understood her, but that was not going to work for me. I needed the situation taken care of as soon as possible.

I went to the school the next day with Kimmy Jo, Kevin Scott, and Karmentrina. Miss Gentile was in her classroom. Children were just starting to come in. I walked over to Miss Gentile holding Kimmy Jo's hand and asked her why she pulled Kimmy Jo's hair and shook her head when she did not know the answer to her math problem.

Miss Gentile was at a loss for words. I said, "I am Mrs. Kearse," and at the same time, I reached over, grabbed a hand full of her hair, and shook her head. The teacher next door came over to see what was going on because the children were running next door to her classroom. Soon Sister Mary Francis showed up and we went into the hallway. Miss Gentile told them both that everything was fine. To make a long story short, Miss Gentile and I became the best of friends. The Catholic school fit my children well after that incident.

I would walk Kimmy Jo, Kevin, and Karmentrina across the College Avenue Bridge, which was more than halfway to school. Things were going well until one day they started coming home from school asking for something to eat. I thought it strange because I gave them money every day to pay for their lunch. It seemed like every time things were going well, something else came up for me to deal with.

Finally, one day I asked Kimmy Jo if they were eating lunch in school.

Kimmy said, "No mom, we do not have any money when we get to school."

I asked why and she told me a big girl was on the other side of the bridge and was taking their money every day by the park before they arrived at the school.

Now you know I was angry as hell. Someone was always pushing my buttons. I asked them why they did not tell me, and Kevin blurted out, "Mom she is a *real big* girl! We are scared of her. The big girl said she would beat us up if we tell our mom."

I had some cuss words in my brain for that, but I stayed calm. I gave them money the next morning. I put their lunch money in their socks. I gave them extra money for the big girl to take from them. I went to the bridge and told Kimmy Jo not to start walking across the bridge until they could not see me. I asked them if they understood and Kimmy Jo said she did. I walked over that bridge, stood on the corner of Pershing Ave and College Ave, and sat on Aunt Ginny and Uncle Herman's steps. Low and behold, here comes a little girl at the streetlight, not too big to me but my kids thought otherwise. I watched her cross the street from the Penn Park and walk up to my children and ask for their lunch money. They gave her their money. Just then I stood up off that porch and walked over to that child, pulled my meat cleaver out of my coat, put it to her throat and told her if she ever tried to take money from my kids again, I would cut her throat. I asked her who her mom was, and she told me. I said I would cut her throat too. Do you understand? Inside I was shaking a little. I knew her mom and I was not trying to deal with her. That little girl never bothered my Kimmy Jo, Kevin, or Karmentrina ever again. In fact, she started walking them home from school. She obviously did not tell her Mom and I was glad about that.

Chapter 24

Building New Relationships and Rekindling Old Relationships

I T WAS NOW SPRING. I was happy to live near all of my family once again. My kids made friends with kids in the neighborhood. I joined a singing group called Freedoms Pride with Linda Dowling, Ted Ritter, and Tammy Kennedy. We sang all around York, Pennsylvania. We were the talk of the town. In our small city, our group was so popular. Once we were booked to open for Jerry Butler, and we opened for the group New Birth. My cousin booked us. William Lee Smallwood and his business partner sponsored R&B shows in the local area. It was a great summer. I never had a babysitting problem. My friends Bucky Branch, Wayne Bailey, Renee, and my two brothers and sometimes my next-door neighbor would keep an eye out for them. They came first; if I did not have a sitter, I would stay at home. My kids loved when Wayne Bailey babysat for me. He taught them about proper meals. I told him to give them vegetable soup and crackers for lunch one day. When I returned home after singing group practice, Karmentrina told me that Wayne said they should never have soup for lunch without a sandwich, something he learned in the home economics books in school. Kevin reminded me that Wayne also told them they needed to have desert at suppertime. That was a bit too much. There were no food stamps back then. Wayne looked at me with a devilish smile.

Hot pants and afros were in style. None of my friends wore bras. We sported the sexy look. The Elks on the west side of town and the American Legion on the east side of town was our hangouts. Everybody and anybody were at the American Legion on Friday nights. We danced to live bands until the joint closed. The Legion is where mom schooled my siblings and me on club life. We knew to never leave our open drink sitting on the table if we got up to dance or go to the bathroom because our drinks could be spiked with drugs. Mom was serious about that because Aunt Alameda's drink was spiked when she was a young woman. It was a time when she and mom were out at a club with friends. Mom said she was never the same after that episode. If you did leave your drink, you ordered another one when you returned and threw the other one away. I was living the single life. I never let a man spend the night at my house. My kids never woke up in the morning to a strange man's face at that time in my life.

One night my next-door neighbor was looking out for my kids. I came home late and had forgotten my key. I did not want to wake up my neighbor, so I walked around to my front door and started knocking on the door and calling Kimmy Jo. After about twenty minutes, Karmentrina came down the stairs. She stood up on the arm of the chair and looked out of the window.

I said, "Bonnie (her nickname Leon gave her), please open the door." I said, "Turn on the outside light" and she did. "It's mom."

She responded, "You look like my mom but that could be a trick."

I said, "Ask me what your grandma's name is," and she did. I said, "Dorothy," and she said, "No. Try again."

I said, "Bonnie, you know it is me." I am outside being pissed because I have to pee. Then I said, "Is her name Nanny?"

She said, "Yep. Okay, you must be my mom." She opened the slide lock quickly but had a hard time with the dead bolt. I finally was in the house. I never forgot the house key again.

Chapter 25

Finding Dottie Mae

SEVERAL SPEAK-EASY JOINTS WHERE FOLKS hung out on Sundays to purchase liquor were available. Liquor was not sold legally on Sundays in the state of Pennsylvania. I never liked those places, but my sister Dottie Mae did. I remember one Sunday morning being at mom's house with Mabel. Mom was worried about Dottie Mae. Mom sent us to one of the popular joints and we found our sister sitting up on a bar stool with a shot glass of VO whiskey in front of her. I did not know how she got up on that bar stool. She was up there and was loaded.

Mabel said, "Midget (Mom called her midget when she was older), get your ass down off of that bar stool. Mom was looking for you."

Midget said, "Mabel, I will get down when I finish this drink."

Mabel gave her a look and she just picked up the shot glass and gulped it down. She wobbled all the way to mom's house. Mom told her, "Keep on going to that speak-easy. One day there are going to be raided and your little short ass will end up jail. I am not coming to get you."

Dottie Mae sat down on mom's sofa and fell asleep. Dottie Mae was a character. She was comfortable living in York. Being a dwarf, no one teased her. Everyone knew her. She was married to Clifton Stewart and separated most of the time due to domestic violence.

I hung out a lot and had many friends who hung out at my house. Many of my friends were gay. Back then, they called gay men funny and gay girls, lesbians. I did not care how a person identified him or herself. A friend is a friend no matter what. I taught my children that. I know now there are many descriptions of sexuality. We hung out playing cards, drinking and getting high. Marijuana was a big thing back then. A nickel bag was the thing back then. I did not smoke it, but I packaged it and got my cut. It was a good summer.

Continuing my education started to be on my mind again. I went ahead and applied to the York Hospital Diplomat Nursing Program and the theoretical classes at York College. My third step to getting on track for my future. I took day classes so I would be in school the same hours as my kids. My mom took care of the kids on my late weekday classes. On Saturday classes, my mom would go to my house to check on them. I had a two-hour class on Saturday. One particular Saturday, my mom walked about two blocks to check on her grandchildren and Kimmy Jo would not let her in. She told her Grandmom that she would get a beating if she let strangers in the house.

Mom told her, "You can let your Grandmom in Kimmy Jo, I am not a stranger."

Mom said Kimmy Jo looked through the window and told her that I said she could not let anyone in the house, no matter what they said. Mom was somewhat upset when Kimmy Jo would not let her in, but she said it was good that she followed my instructions. I explained to Kimmy Jo that the next time she could only let her Nanny in the house.

I did well in my nursing rotations, but I could not pass any classes at York College. All tests were essay type questions, and I could never get on the same page with my instructors. I complained to Lee, and he told me to take a class at Penn State York Campus. I took his advice, took chemistry, and received B in that class. I decided I was just not good at essay type examinations. I disappointedly dropped out after two quarters. School was now on the back burner again, and I started working again. I saved a little money every payday so I could give my kids allowance. They loved getting their allowance, mostly change to make it look like it was a lot. One day when they received their allowance, Karmentrina wanted to walk around the corner to Eddie's corner store with Keenan. I walked them to the store and waited outside on the corner talking with some friends. When she and Keenan came out of the store, Karmentrina had a large bag of candy and Keenan had a little bag of candy. I questioned Keenan, like where is the rest of your money?

He said, "Mommy I gave the man in the store all of my money."

I asked him if he gave his sister any money and he said, "Mommy, Karmen gave me her big nickels for my little dimes so I could have more money." I went into the store and got change for a dollar. Five nickels, 1 quarter and 4 dimes, 10 pennies and walked home and sat them down to the kitchen table and explained to all of them the difference in the coins. I made Karmentrina give some of her candy to Keenan. I scolded her. She teared up a little and started to suck her thumb. Karmentrina could make tears show up in a flash. At age four, she knew the difference. Keenan did not at age three. I knew then I had a slick one on my hands. I often gave Karmentrina a pass because she was a sickly child with her asthma. I walked many times from our house to the York Hospital allergy clinic. At times I would have to walk both ways and other times I had just enough for a one-way bus trip. I would carry her on my back until I was too tired to go further. It was about twelve long blocks. I had a driver's license, but I did not have a car.

One night about 1 am, she woke me up having difficult time breathing and had a croup cough. I called the York Hospital Emergency room and asked for Dr. Mulligan, a doctor I worked with in the emergency room recently. They paged him, and I told him what was going on. He told me to take her in the bathroom and run the hot water to get as much steam as I could. Her breathing became better after about 25 minutes. We went to sleep in my bed. She slept very well. When I woke up Karmentrina was no longer in my bed. I felt wet under the covers and when I pulled them back; I was soaked and so was my bed. Karmentrina had wet the bed, got up and went and changed into clean dry pajamas, went back to sleep in her own bed. That was slick. The next morning at three in the morning, Dr. Mulligan called me. I was sleeping so well. He asked how Karmentrina was doing, and I really appreciated that. I said to him, that was yesterday morning. She is okay this morning. He responded; "I know you did not call me back to let me know that she was okay. He taught me then that it was important to follow through when you say you will. Dr. Mulligan and I remained friends for years.

A few years back when we lived on Penn Street before moving to Philadelphia, Karmentrina fell out of her crib and fractured her right jaw. That is how I first met Dr. Mulligan. Karmentrina had to be in the hospital for weeks. I worked at the York Hospital at that time. All of the staff on the pediatric ward spoiled her. During my duty hours, I would visit her quite a bit. Leon would visit and sit with her in the evenings. We took turns on the weekends because we could not take the children on the pediatric ward. That was okay; Karmentrina did not even cry for us when we left her. She had all kinds of toys in her crib. I had purchased a porta crib for her. My mom did not trust it. I should have listened to her. The latch at the top came undone when Karmentrina leaned on it and she fell out. That was a stressful time for me.

I later started working again in a private practice mental health clinic. Lord knows I did not need to do that. I started delving into the mental unknown. I was trying to practice with out-of-body experiments. I sat through some classes and thought I could try mentally concentrating on my spirit leaving my body. One evening after work after I had put the children to bed, I thought I would try it. I turned off all of the lights in my living room and lay down on the couch. It was very quiet and still. I asked my spirit to rise out of my body. Nothing was happening. I kept still and continued to concentrate. I could feel and see myself leaving my body. I was so frightened; I could not wake myself up. I could feel tears in my eyes and see my inner body looking down at me. I started to hear someone knocking on the door, but I could not wake up. The knocking became louder and I finally woke up, very shaken. It was Bucky and Wayne stopping by. They looked at me and asked if I had been crying. I denied it saying that I was just trying to sleep. The next day I put my two-week resignation in. I was only there a few months. I was tired of job hunting; however, I was not going to be playing with the unknown.

I told Mary I needed another job and she told me that her friend PeeWee told about a restaurant looking for people to bus tables. I did not know about that. I was not feeling, busting tables. We did go and apply. Things were going good. It was quite a hustle and some evenings our feet would be killing us. One evening while we were waiting for our ride, Mary said she was not going back after that evening shift because those white people were not giving us any good tips. When she quit that evening, I quit too; I was not going to be the only black person in that restaurant bussing tables. Lord knows that I was tired of job-hopping. I knew something would come up again as it always did. I knew then that I would have to job hunt on my own because Mary never stayed on a job to long.

I was very active as a Head Start parent and attended all parent meetings. The director of the program asked me if I would like to be on the parent teacher board, and I accepted the invitation. There was no money in it, but I was able to travel a lot. One such trip was via an airplane to Chicago, Illinois, which would be my very first airplane ride. I was so nervous just thinking about being on an airplane. As the time grew close, I wanted to bail out, but my mom told me to go on that trip. She told me it might just be interesting. One never knows whom they might meet and or the new experiences it could offer. There were about five of us scheduled to go on that trip. When we met up at a parent's house to get our ride to the airport in Harrisburg, one of the male parents said to me, "Sandra, you know one out of three airplanes have been known to wreck and this is the third United Airlines plane to fly this month."

I looked at him as if I just saw a ghost and the director told him to stop frightening me. She looked at me and said, "Sandra do not pay him any at attention."

I was so happy when that airplane landed but knew I would be flying back on another plane. I was praying to myself, *Lord please do not let that airplane be number three.*

After many meetings and talking with many persons, I continued to look for someone who could help me to succeed in being a spokesperson for those who could not speak for themselves. I had a voice that demanded attention and I knew it. I soon met a wonderful young woman named Caroline Sexton who lived in The Parkway Housing Projects. Carolyn was an amazing woman and I wanted to be just like her when I grew up: Speak with a command in my voice and make it so no one could deny me the outcome I was after. We sat in her kitchen and she told me what her volunteer job was. At that time, she was working with a black female human rights attorney from Philadelphia. She told me that she worked on welfare rights issues. I started going to meetings with Caroline in Philadelphia. I went with her to the York County Welfare Office. I watched her fight for clients who had their stipends threatened. Finally, a case came up that she thought I could handle. Caroline wanted me to be the mediator for a client. I told her I did not think I could do it without her there. She told me it was now or never because I had watched her more than enough times.

That morning came up for me to help this client (her name is private information). I was up early; the meeting was not until the early afternoon. I had to use the bathroom about one hundred times that morning just being nervous. Caroline told me the goal of the game was to be able to interpret the welfare office policies and procedures better than they could themselves. The client and I walked out of the office with smiles on our faces. The client was getting her current stipend as well as her back money. I liked fighting cases for clients. I can do this.

Summer was approaching; it was time to start hanging out again with friends. The singing group was practicing again, and I was all in. One Friday evening my bestie, Renee Ware, stopped by for us to walk around the corner to the bar. I met a person there, Bruce Wright, who invited me to a party the next evening, which was a Friday. My friend said she knew him. I saw him around before. The next day I showed up to the address that he gave me, and he opened the door. I asked where the people were. He said it is a surprise party. People will to start showing up soon. Okay, about twenty-five minutes rolled right on by and no one had showed up. Now I am concerned; Renee told me she knew him. I finally asked what is going on, there is no party, right. He affirmed my suspicions and said, "I just wanted to be with you. I see you out at the Legion all the time, but you never have the time of day for me."

I told him to open the door; I was ready to go, and he did. He walked me all the way across the bridge from George Street to Codorus Street Projects. Long walk home. We started to see each other and became close later on. The talk gets around town quickly when a man shows up at your house in the projects.

I just happened to run into Leon at the corner bar one afternoon and he said, "I heard you are going out with my cousin."

I said, "What?"

He said, "Bruce Wright. I wish you good luck."

I was hoping I would not need that. Things went very well until I found out that Bruce had children to a maniac girl. That girl called my house every other day looking for him. Most days he was not at my house. That was just what I got for not having a private number. We hung in there for about eleven months. I really felt close to Bruce and thought we might be able to pull this relation off, if I could only deal with the maniac woman who bore his children and needed pampers and milk every time I turned around. It just became worse.

January nineteen hundred seventy two my cousin Douglas Smallwood (Doug) came home on leave from the Air Force and had a friend Ace with him. Doug brought him by my house to meet me after they had been running around town for a while meeting Doug's friends. I was one of the popular singers in town, so everyone hung out at my house. I said hello to him, he was light skinned, cute, slanted-eyed brother who kept giving me a flirtatious look behind Doug's back.

I said, "You are staring."

He said, "When Doug told me he wanted me to meet his cool cousin Lou, I didn't realize he was talking about a girl."

I said, "Surprise, I am a female, not one of his boy cousins."

They did not stay very long but returned about two weeks later because Ace wanted to see me again. He told me the orange hot pants, halter-top and my short afro cut did grab his attention. I saw no need to tell him anything about Bruce because nothing was really going on right now. In addition, I was trying to break away from Bruce Wright because of his baby mama drama. Bruce was a wonderful person and meant much to my kids and me.

I remember one time when he wanted to take Kimmy Jo and Kevin fishing. I was a little skeptical because of the bad experience I had while fishing with my dad years ago in the Susquehanna River under the old Columbia Bridge. I did allow him to take them. They returned about three hours later and Kimmy Jo came running into the house yelling, "Mommy, Kevin almost drowned; Kevin fell into the water."

Bruce and Kevin were right behind her and Bruce told me what happened. He said that Kevin was standing on the rock he put him on holding his fishing pole. He was fishing right close to him when Kevin slipped off the rock. He said Kimmy Jo started screaming that Kevin was in the water. He told me he ran over to him, and he was treading water and hanging in there when he got to him. He said he jumped in and got Kevin to the dry ground. I said thank God I paid for them swimming lessons at the YMCA. I used to go to the YMCA to watch them swim. Kevin would never jump off the diving board, but Kimmy Jo, at age four, loved jumping off the diving board.

It would not be long when Doug and three of his Air Force friends stopped by my house. This time it was Ace, Paige, and Charles Whatley. They were all dressed as if they were hustlers with their gold chains, hats, and fly clothing. They were having a talk about a tire issue they had on the way up from Washington, DC. They decided to go to the gas station out on East Market Street where they could get the tire fixed or something. Doug told me I could come along if I wanted. My friends who were hanging with me at my house then were cool with it for my kids were home. I did join them. When we arrived at the gas station, everyone got out of the car except Ace and me. Ace was trying to see how far he could go with me in that back seat. I stopped him and asked him if he thought I was easy. Just about that time Doug opened the back car door and told Ace it was time for him to stop playing Casanova and help them with the tire situation. That was on time. I was not feeling his *"Romen hands and Russian"* fingers.

When they finished fixing the tire, they took me home and headed back down the road to Andrews Air Force Base. My girl, Renee Ware, stopped by that evening late. Renee practically lived with me. I told her about Ace, how cute he was and that he was in the Air Force too. Renee said, "Speak to me girl." I told her that I thought he liked me, but I am not sure about him. He is just a little too cool for me. Like city slick. Even though we had, no social media there was already quite a few girls who had their eyes set on Ace. The buzzes were in process. Thanks to Doug for introducing him around town and not making me the first stop when they hit town for the first time, my competition in the street was already brewing.

Not too long after I told Renee about Ace, he and Doug showed up. Renee was in the kitchen cooking when they knocked on the door. She invited them in. I heard her say what's up to Doug. I could hear her, as the project housing was not soundproof. Renee came running upstairs telling me my cousin Doug was downstairs, and he has this fine, super fly, high yellow, slanted-eyed brother with him. I asked her if he had black curly hair and she responded, "Sure does, and girl." I told her to back off because that was Ace. We now had been talking on the phone almost every day.

Another late Friday evening to my surprise, Aaron showed up without Doug. He knocked on the door and I answered. I asked where Doug was and he said he just dropped him off at my house. He was to call him when he was ready to leave. At this time, I told him I had kids and that he could meet them if he wanted too. They were asleep upstairs, but I told him we could still go upstairs to see them. We went upstairs and I opened the door to my daughters' room. In that room was four little girls sleeping. Then we went to my son's room. There were three little boys sleeping. Then I took him to my bedroom and my niece, Tracey, was under my bed sleeping, her favorite place when she stayed with me. We proceeded downstairs and when we sat down in the kitchen, Ace had this strange look on his face, like what did I get myself into with this girl. He said to me, "Are they all of your kids?" I went to the fridge, took out a bottle of Boons Farm wine, and was ready to pour us a drink.

He put a stop to the wine and said, "No," and pulled out his flask. "This calls for Notty Head (Seagram's gin)."

I told him to drink that and I would drink the wine. I was feeling that he was ready to call for his ride now.

I said, "Relax, I only have four children. They are Kimmy Jo, Kevin Scott, Karmentrina Schevelle, and Keenan Wynn. My sister, Mary, went to New York for the weekend. She sent her kids down to my house after school today with a note that read, 'Hey Sandi, went to NY be back Sunday morning'." I had no choice but to keep my sister's kids.

It was getting very late, so I invited him to spend the night. He had a backpack with him, so I assumed that he was counting on that invitation. Ace phoned Doug and told him he would get with him in the morning. That night, Aaron told me he didn't mind kids because he lived with his older sister Kaye Tompkins (Rest in Peace) and her five kids while in high school and before leaving to go into the U. S. Air Force. The next morning, Saturday morning, before the kids woke up, he went to the corner and brought breakfast for all of us. He cooked eggs, bacon, and toast. The kids were wondering who he was. Karmentrina my nosiest little girl asked him if he was my boyfriend. He told her to ask your mom. Kimmy Jo chimed in and said to Karmentrina, "Brucie is mom's boyfriend." Out of the mouth of babes! I just left it alone.

I asked him if he wanted to spend another night. I had eight kids to deal with until my sister returned home on Sunday morning. He said he would love to spend another night. That night after all the kids were asleep, we watched television for some time. Then we went upstairs to go to bed. We walked into my room and Ace sat down on the side of the bed and started to take off his shoes. I stopped him and said, "I do not think you want to get undressed just yet." He responded, "Why?"

I walked around to the other side of my bed away from the door and looked under my bed for Tracey.

162

I said, "Let's go Tracey." I hugged her and took her to her bed in the girl's room. That night we talked a lot about who we were. I asked him what his real name was. I said I noticed that Doug and your friends call you Ace, The Godfather. I said you are the smallest of the crew; your nickname means what? He responded my real name is Aaron Edward.

I said, "For real?" He said, "Yes." I told him my real name was Sandra Lee Kearse. I told him I preferred Sandra to Lou. I told him he would hear many call me that and it was ok. I told him I would call him Aaron because I did not want to be on the same level as his friends. He said, "Sandra it is."

We discussed many things that night. It felt like we were starting a relationship. I was going to have to break my connection with Bruce Wright. I did not mention him or anyone else to Aaron yet. It was not in my heart to hurt Bruce, but our relationship had to end. My mom went through that with all the women my dad was running. I saw her pain for years.

One Friday night when Aaron came to visit Tommy, a friend, knocked on my door. Aaron and I were in my bedroom watching television, and I looked out of the window. I was once again thinking to myself, *damn it*. Tommy kept on knocking and Aaron asked if that was my man. I explained the situation to him and that by no means was he my man. He had been trying to pursue me for some time. He is a married man. I told Aaron that I would not allow myself to be in that kind of situation. He told me to open the door then. I asked, "What if he starts something; he is much bigger than you are." Aaron made it clear to me not to let his size fool me. He was not worried about him.

We went downstairs. I opened the door and Aaron was sitting in a chair at the kitchen table. Tommy walked in and saw him. He said, "Oh you have company."

I said; "I do."

He said, "No problem I was just stopping by to see you."

I introduced them and Tommy left. Aaron said, "Now that was not so bad was it?"

I guess word was in the street that I had a new friend. Tommy never stopped over again or telephoned me. Okay, now I know why he was nicknamed the God Father.

Sunday morning about 11 am, Mary came to my house to get her kids. I introduced her to Aaron; he was sitting on the back porch smoking a cigarette. Mary could not wait to go to my mom's house and tell her about him. Lord, she had to stop by Mabel's house too. Doug came to pick Aaron up about two pm because they had to get back to Andrews Air Force Base for duty. I took a walk with my kids to mom's house. You know Mary was still there gossiping about my new friend. I told mom he said he was 22 years old.

Mary chimed in and said, "No damn way Mom. He looked like a little kid. He is not anybody's 22 years old!" Sandi is so stupid; she wants a man so bad. She will believe anything at this point.

I said, "He showed me a military identification card that proves he is twenty-two, smart-ass. Mind your own damn business and the next time you want me to watch your kids for the weekend, come, and ask me. You are just jealous." I decided I needed to leave mom's house because they were all trying to be in my business.

During the week, Aaron and I had many telephone conversations. He asked if he could come up for the weekend. He said he was going to take a bus because Doug was not coming home for the weekend. I told him it would be okay, but that I had singing group practice on Saturday. He said he did not mind and still wanted to come. He arrived Friday evening and took a taxicab to my house. He had gifts for all of my children. He looked after them on Saturday when I had practice. When I returned home from practice, the kids were all excited. I could hardly get in the door when Karmentrina ran over to me and said, "Mom your boyfriend took us to McDonalds!" Kevin and Keenan chimed in with *we got toys too*. Oh, but Kimmy Jo was not buying it. Kimmy Jo was quiet, protective of her mommy. I asked him how he took the kids to McDonalds because he had no car. Aaron told me that one could do a lot with money. He told me he walked around the corner where everyone hangs out and asked someone to take him and his kids to McDonalds. I thought, okay then. Kimmy Jo warmed up to Aaron after they all started getting packages from the Fed-Ex truck. They were the only kids in the projects getting packages from the Fed-Ex truck every week. My kids started looking for that Fed-Ex truck, like me and my siblings used to look out the window for my dad, William, to come home on the truck. Only they did not have to worry about anyone's bad mood. The packages just kept on coming. One day my mom was at the house, witnessed a big delivery, and asks who was sending the packages and who was getting the packages. I hardly had time to answer her when Kevin Scott said, "Mom's new Air Force boyfriend."

Kimmy Jo had to add her comment and said, "He sends us boxes all the time."

My mom just gave me a look. Keenan and Kevin ran to the toy box and brought out the little army men and toy army trucks he sent to them. Karmentrina yells to my mom, "He is rich Nanny!"

I said, "He is not rich Karmentrina, he has a job. He is in the military."

The next time Aaron came for a visit, I took him to my mom's house along with my kids to meet her and Mister Bill, whom I have always considered was a father to me.

All of my sisters just happened to be there. Bucky and Wayne showed up soon after we arrived there. Mom was in the kitchen cooking and Mary was helping her. Mr. Bill kept asking mom when the food was going to be ready because he was hungry. He called out to the kitchen, "Dorothy, how long we got?"

Mom said, "You can get a couple of hotdogs Bill, if you are that hungry."

Mr. Bill went to the icebox, took out a couple of cold hotdogs, sat down to the table, and started eating. He was half ass drunk and offered Aaron a cold raw hotdog and he accepted the offer and ate it. Mr. Bill said, "That's my kind of man!"

That afternoon, all went well. Aaron really gelled with my family. Dinner was done. Mary and I volunteered to clean up the kitchen. I had the hard part. I was washing the dishes and she was drying the dishes while running her mouth.

Mary said, "He got you fooled. I do not care what identification he showed you. There is no way in the world that he is over 21 years of age."

"Mary, we had this conversation before and I didn't say anything back to you, out of respect. Whatever age he happens to be, he is mine and my children love him. Are you all right with that my sister? If not, I do not give a damn about what you or anyone else thinks."

The house started emptying out; all of my sisters went home. Aaron was hanging out on the front porch-smoking cigarette with my brothers, Bucky and Wayne. Wayne came home with Bucky one evening on a weekend and Bucky asked Mom if he could spend the night. Mom allowed him to stay overnight. The next night he asked to spend the night again and mom if it is okay with his mom it is okay with me. Bucky tried it again for the third night and mom asked where his mom is. Wayne told mom he lived in a house by himself. Wayne told mom that his mom stayed with her boyfriend. Mom did not fall for that, so she called Wayne's mom to see what was going on. After mom finished talking to Wayne's mom, she was so irritated and could not believe what she heard from Wayne's mom. To make a long story short, Wayne started living with mom, Mr. Bill, and Bucky from that point on.

Aaron, the kids and I walked a few blocks back to the projects to my house. It was still early. A few of my friends came over and they put their money together and brought some beer. We played spades until the wee hours. I finally kicked everyone out and we all went to bed. The kids had fallen asleep on the floor in front of the television. Waking them up was always a chore. Later on in bed, Aaron told me he liked my family, especially my little sister, Dottie Mae. He said she cornered him and asked for a couple of dollars to buy a bottle of beer from Eddie's Bar. I believed him because Dottie Mae was always good at getting a couple of dollars from one of us sisters. I remember a time at 480 Codorus Street when I saved up about five dollars in dimes to buy myself some new marbles. Somehow, my money came up missing. Mabel and Dottie Mae were the only two who shared a room with me. I was so proud of saving and told mom about it. They probably overheard our conversation. At about that time, Mabel and Dottie Mae had a bunch of candy and cupcakes they brought from the corner store. They both were sitting out in the back yard on the wooden steps just enjoying themselves. I told mom back then that they took my money. Neither one of them would confess to stealing my stash. Since mom did not know who was telling the truth she did not punish either of them. I was so mad. This was one time I wished William had been there. William would have beaten both of them. They both would have deserved to be whipped. Those were the days of Codorus Street.

Things with Aaron were becoming very serious. I started going to Washington, DC every other weekend and sometimes during the week. I looked forward to the bus rides because I was going to see my new Air Force boyfriend. We went to so many malls because I fell in love with the huge Springfield Mall. We went to Iverson Mall on the regular because Aaron liked buying his clothing at Cavaliers and his shoes at Stacey Adams and Johnson and Murphy Shoes. On one of those shopping events, Aaron purchased a pair of shoes at Stacy Adams shoe store for sixty-five dollars. There I was thinking to myself for that price, I could have bought a pair of shoes for my children and me. Do not get me wrong -- I liked the shopping sprees because he pampered me and purchased things for me and he always said we have to buy something for the kids. My kind of guy. Back in the day, my mom had to save for everything. Money was usually tight. I learned from her. I was living off my social security pension and my part-time job and with rent reduction in the projects; my kids and I were doing okay. I was thinking like my kids were: *Is he from a rich family or something?*

I had not meant anyone from Aaron's family. He only told me that his oldest brother, Michael, was in the Air Force and had encouraged him to go into the Air Force as well. I did not know much about the military back then, but Aaron and Doug were never broke and they were always dressed like Super Fly and Shaft, both characters from Blaxpoitation films in the seventies. They both had two stripes on their uniform sleeve. I wanted to ask him about the money, but I did not want to lose my money tree. If you were never in the financial struggle, you will never understand this. We went to the movies, restaurants, Atlantic City Boardwalk where I had never been before, and this was before casinos. We had lunch at a large crowded restaurant. When lunch was over, Aaron left a five-dollar tip. When he got up and turned his back for few seconds, I picked up the five dollars and put down a dollar. Walking down the boardwalk later, I told him. He laughed and asked did I think that was too much and I said I sure did. That is why I left a dollar. I handed him the five and said you owe me a dollar. Aaron said from now on, he would ask me what the tip should be. I said, "Good deal." This was actually the relationship I never had, dating for real. One memory that always stuck with me was Aaron would always hold my hand when we were out. I felt like a young teenager and carefree. This was different from when I and many other teen moms were pursued by predators. We could not go to the places our male predators would go to because we were children; the relationship had to be hidden or in the dark. Many teen moms had moms whom were embarrassed or just could not afford to care for their teen daughter and her baby, sent their babies to live with other family members to raise, or gave them to other people that the family knew wanted a baby. Those mothers may not have thought about how this would affect their daughters for their entire life.

One of my friends who had a baby as a teen contracted some type of infection after the birth of her baby. She went back and forth to the York Hospital and one day she never left the hospital alive. All of the teen moms knew about this and felt bad about it. Teenage girls were children having children. Their bodies not developed well enough for childbearing. Childbirth was a physical deterioration to our bodies and a mental, emotional burden to our survival. If you did not have a family to support system, especially a strong mom, your chances of being a good mom was at risk.

Aaron and I double dated with his friends in the Washington, DC area frequently. He told me that if I ever felt uncomfortable around his friends to let him know for they would no longer be his friends. I met several of his friends and their girlfriends and had no issues with anyone. He showed me some of the many monuments in Washington DC. The only time I ever heard about Washington, DC was when young girls from York were applying for government jobs in the District. Grownups in York always advised their children to apply for government jobs in the Nation's Capital because of job longevity, benefits, and retirement. This was not happening in York, Pennsylvania.

Another time, we went on a jazz cruise on the Potomac and it was nice, but I was not into jazz. I told him and he said, let me introduce you to jazz. I could not swim and did not like being on the water. However, it was a good experience. We had been hanging together for a while now, and I had not met any of his family yet. I was hoping that he was not ashamed to introduce me to his family. Then again, I thought about his situation. He did not drive and his family lived in Pittsburgh, Roanoke, Virginia, and North Carolina.

Chapter 26

Road Block....Time To Put the Brakes On!

I WAS A BUSY WOMAN THAT summer. Singing practice and going to see Aaron all the time. One day I went to singing practice and one of my first cousins, Terry Lee, was staying with me for a few days. I was only at practice for a few hours. When I returned home, there was a lot of commotion in my back yard. A car had hit Keenan. He ended up with just a few bruises. The person who hit him was there also and shook up. He said; "Your little boy ran into the street out of nowhere." I told him not to worry. Leon heard about it and came to my house and invited himself in and started preaching somewhat. He was right on a few things. I needed to be home more often with my own kids. Lord knows I would have been truly broken beyond repair if something horrible would have happened to any of my kids. Leon was with me throughout my pregnancy with Keenan and cared for him like a father.

That was a weekday. I was supposed to go to visit Aaron that following Saturday morning. Aaron telephoned me a day after the car hit Keenan. I told him what happened. He said that he was sorry to hear of that news. I told him that we would have to change how much and when we saw each other in the future. He agreed. I told him that I would visit him only one time per month, but he could visit us as many times as he would like to visit. He continued to spoil my kids. If they did not get Fed-Ex Truck deliveries, he would bring them goodies or gifts when he visited. Doug stopped by one Friday evening alone and told me that Ace would not be able to come until the next week as planned because he had duty. Doug had a small round white color television that hung from the wall that Aaron sent for me to put in my bedroom. I told my cousin that it was nice of Aaron to do that. Doug said he is into you, Sandi. I smiled. I certainly did appreciate that TV hanging from my bedroom ceiling, color too. Then Doug handed me a large white sealed envelope and said that Aaron told him to give it to me to hold until next week. I asked Doug to lift my dresser up so I could slide the envelope under the dresser until he showed up the following week. Doug and I chatted for a few minutes and then he left. He had not been home yet and said to me, "You know how it is in York, if someone sees me and tells Yvette I am in town before she sees me, well, that would not be good (Laughter)."

Later on that evening, my girl, Renee, showed up and I told her all about it. I told her I was dying to open that envelope, but I told Doug I would keep it safe until Aaron arrived next week. Renee said we are not going to do anything but look inside of the envelope. I told her it was sealed. She said we would steam it open and seal it back when we check it out. It took a few minutes for us to get the envelope out from under the dresser because Doug had pushed it back pretty far. I had a long knife and used it to push the envelope to the side so I could get my fingers on it to pull it out. We both went down to the kitchen and heated a small pot of water until it began to produce steam. We steamed open the envelope. Our eyes almost fell out of our heads. I never saw so many hundred dollar bills in my life. It was one thousand dollars. Lord Jesus. We put them all back into the envelope and sealed it back closed. I carried it back upstairs where Renee and I managed to slide it back under the dresser but not as far back as Doug placed it. I looked at

Renee and said, "What the heck???" Renee said, "You know his boys and your cousin call him God Father for a reason."

The following Friday evening finally was here and Aaron came for the weekend. He took a late greyhound bus and then on arrival to York, he had to get a taxicab. It was late when he showed up that Friday night. The kids were already in bed. Aaron came inside; he hugged me and asked if Doug left something for him, and I said, "Yes, it is upstairs." We went upstairs to my bedroom, and I thanked him for the television. It hung right above my long dresser. I told him the envelope was under the dresser and he would have to get it because the dresser was too heavy for me to move. He moved towards the dresser, I stepped back away from it a little. He took out the envelope, handed it to me, and said this is for you and the kids. I opened it and pretended as if I was in shock. I started to count it, even though I already knew the amount. I hugged him and thanked him for the gifts for my kids and me, saying to myself, I really needed that money. That was a good sex night. I never once asked where that money came from. I thought about the two pair of shoes I had on layaway for Kimmy Jo and Kevin Scoot. They both wore high-top shoes from the Stride Rite Shoe Store to help correct their rolled ankles. I thought about the play I wanted to take my kids to the following month. I thought of enough reasons why I needed that money without any questions asked. I also remember my mom telling my siblings and me *"Ain't nothing free."*

Chapter 27

Hurricane Agnes June 14, 1972
– June 23, 1972

I T WAS MY TWENTY-THIRD BIRTHDAY when Hurricane Agnes hit York, Pennsylvania. It was hot and humid all day and it seemed like it rained forever. That Wednesday morning of June 14, 1972, I woke up to clouds and rain. It was raining so hard for days on edge. Local television news kept talking about all of the rain we were getting in York, Pennsylvania but the local television stations did not report any news about a hurricane or an impending flood. It rained off and on for days until Tropical Storm Agnes arrived in York on Monday, June 19, 1972 and brought severe flooding by Thursday, June 22, 1972 — forty-seven years ago. The destruction that began as a Category 1 hurricane swept up the East Coast of the United States and was of such magnitude that the name was retired from future use, according to York Daily Record archives. (Google search for Hurricane Agnes of York, Pennsylvania for photos and the story.)

That night, the water covered the Penn Street Bridge, about one-half block from 351 Stone Avenue; my friends were in my kitchen playing cards. I kept looking out of my back-kitchen door to see how close the water was. The rain had risen over the street curb. I decided to walk that half of block as I did several times that day and evening to see how far the water had risen under the bridge. I was shocked to see that I could not even see the bridge. The water was now covering the bridge. I ran back to my house, it was very late, and woke up my four kids. I grabbed a bag of important papers and my kids and headed for the back-kitchen door. My phone rang and it was Aaron; I could hardly hear him. The phone had a lot of static. I told him quickly about what was going on and that I would talk to him another time. He said, "Be safe Sandra." I said, "I plan to." I threw my door keys on the table and told my friends to lock up when they left. I told them I was taking my kids to my mom's house. They all laughed and told me to calm down, there was not going to be no flood. I yelled on the way out, "When you people get your weatherman license let me know. I am the weatherman now." I packed up my kids in their travel mode. Clothes on their backs!

When my kids and I stepped into my backyard, the water was almost above my Kimmy Jo and Kevin's knees. I placed Kimmy Jo on my right side and Kevin Scott on my left side and told them to hold on to my side pockets and not to let go no matter what. I had Karmentrina on my back and I was carrying Keenan. My sneakers were soaked before we started to walk. We started trudging through the water, and I was very much afraid. My little Kevin kept asking me if we were going to drown. I told him not if I could help it. He kept on asking repeatedly and Kimmy Jo finally said to him we are not going to drown Kevin so be quiet. The water was coming down so hard, I could hardly see and it felt like Karmentrina was slipping off my back. I had to stop for a few seconds and reposition her legs around my waist. I put her feet inside the band of my shorts to help her to hang on. We waded about one block to Mary's house. I could see the light on in her front room. I banged on the door and she yelled, "Who is banging on my door?" I said, "It's your sister." I pushed opened the door and I ran in with my kids. The water was now over her first step of three stairs. Mary was sitting in her comfortable chair smoking a cigarette and watching television. I was tired and so were Kimmy Jo and Kevin. Mary looked at us; all drenched from the rain, and asked what was going on? I told her I thought we were having a flood. The Codorus creek had risen, and the Penn Street Bridge was not visible. Water was covering the bridge. I told her to look outside and she did. Mary went into panic mode, started crying and running around as if she was nuts.

Mary said, "Wait for me; I have to get my kids!" I told her to calm down wake up her kids and get them to safety. I told her that I was going to mom's house, another three blocks away but uphill from where we were. I told her again to calm down; we are both moms who have to get our kids to a safe place. I left her saying I would, "see you when I see you." We hiked that hill to my mom's house, which was going away from the floodwaters and were safe. I now was able to let Karmentrina walk. Mom was listening to the news and heard we were getting floodwaters. Mr. Bill drove my kids and me to Mabel's house out by the York Hospital. It was quite a distance from the floodwaters. He drove back home to get my Mom and they drove to Parkway Housing Projects to Miss Ruthie Bank's house where they were safe.

Telephone service went down so we could not call anyone for days. Mabel's radio did work so we could hear most of what was going on in the flood areas. My kids and I stayed at Mabel's house overnight. We were crowded because she had her own kids, Larry, Trevorr, and Elmer (Minky). All of the kids finally went to sleep, but Mabel and I were worried about our other sisters. Our Bucky and Wayne lived with Mom, so we knew they were just fine.

The next morning Mabel and I decided to walk about twenty blocks or so to the College Avenue Bridge, which was higher than the

Penn Street Bridge to see what we could see. We also wanted to find out if there was any news about persons who lived in the flood areas. We wanted to know if everyone was able to get out. We found out that the city sent buses into the area to evacuate everyone in the flood areas to churches and other family member's homes not affected. We could see that the floodwater was covering the Codorus Street Project houses almost to the second-floor levels. It was such a site. It was like something out of the Bible. We had all lost so much. I did not have much but it was all that I had. There were many folks out there all wondering how we would survive this. We saw some men riding in boats to get through the water. That was just craziness. We walked back to Mabel's house. We still did not hear from our sisters. The next day I went to my mom's house who had returned home. Mr. Bill came for us.

A few days later, the water had all went away and left all of its trash behind, to include but not limited to mud, dead rats, old tires, and all kinds of trash. Bucky and Wayne caught up with me at mom's house and walked down to the Codorus Street Projects to see what shape my house was in. It was a complete mess. There were many of the neighbors doing the same thing, seeing for the first time the damage and destruction. It was about two feet of mud on the first floor. Slowly, some of my friends started coming out of the woodwork, dressed up in 1920's garb. I laughed and asked, "Who gave you the clothing?"

My friend Wendell said, "The Salvation Army." He told me he saw my sister Mary with her kids getting clothing. I was happy to hear that she was okay. Lee Smallwood stopped by my house to check on me. He came into the house and said, "Damn." We did a walkthrough with Renee, Bucky, and Wayne. Furniture strewn about, fridge on its side full of muddy water and the pantry was indescribable. The living room furniture was water soaked and not useable any longer. We walked through the mud to the second-floor level. The water and mud did not make it to the top of the steps. I was so grateful that all of our three bedrooms were intact, just as we left them. After that, Lee decided that we needed to get all of the mud out of the house as soon as possible for it could cause illness due to contaminants.

Lee took Bucky and Wayne with him to get supplies. They returned with shovels, brooms, bleach, and a water hose. Only brown water was coming out of the water hose. Lee said we will use the water to get the mud out and hopefully by the next day or so we would have clean water. My friend Wayne Bailey from South Newberry Street came by to check on me and saw us cleaning up and jumped right in to help us with the cleanup effort. He said his family's house was under water.

It was so hot and humid in the house. In addition, mosquitoes were everywhere outside. We did not have a choice. We opened all of the windows and started shoveling and sweeping out the mud. It seemed like we would never be done. Lee, Bucky, and Wayne dragged the couches out of the house and the coffee table I kept. That was not going anywhere, because my mom gave it to me. We kept the fridge and the kitchen table and chairs. Next was the water hose challenge. Lee hooked up the water hose and started to wash out the rest of the mud from the stairs down through the entire house. Then Lee hosed down the fridge after Wayne and Bucky put it outside. Then we cleaned it with bleach. We kept the fridge outside until it dried out. It was bright and sunny outside. It was easy to realize that forty days and forty nights of water could swallow up the whole world.

We cleaned for hours then just hung out talking about the flood that we all just experienced. As the days came and went, things gradually came back to order as we knew it. My kids and I remained at my mom's house for about two weeks. Renee and I stayed at my house. One morning Renee went to check on her mom, her sister Wanda, and her brother

Wendell on South Penn Street. She was gone for hours. When she returned in a taxicab, she had groceries. I went outside to help her. When we finished, I asked her where she got the money for all of that food. Her exact words, "Girlfriend, the American Red Cross is given out grocery store vouchers for food to families and money for furniture. I went with my mom. I filled out the paperwork and told them I had three children. Girl you better go and get yours before the money runs out, you would not be telling a lie. You have four kids and we need that food!"

I certainly went to the American Red Cross filled out my paperwork and received my vouchers. Of course, I went grocery store shopping too. Mr. Bill took me shopping, but I did not have any gas money. He told me not to worry just buy him a jar of pickled pig feet. That was a deal! I got him two jars. I purchased all of the food I could get and took it home. Weeks later, government workers came through offering relief grants. I filled out my paperwork and received three thousand dollars.

That evening Renee wanted to go to a rent party she heard about. Five dollars to get in. Everyone needed money during those days. She invited me and I went with her to the party. The party was at a house in the projects close to where we were. That party was so crowded; we could hardly squeeze into the house. The music was loud. I saw my cousin, Charles Smallwood, across the room all loud. He looked up and saw me yelling, "Hey cuz, what's up with you?" Renee seemed to disappear for a few minutes and then returned.

Renee said, "I just scored."

I am like, "What do you mean you just scored?"

She explained she had some black beauties. I had no idea what that was. She told me, "Girl they will give you some energy, which we need after all we have been through with this flood crisis." I was thinking we are past the flood crisis now. Reluctantly I swallowed one of the black beauties, as did she.

Shortly after I took that pill, it seemed like everything was going in fast motion. I was a little worried and said that to Renee. I did not want to be having an overdose. I had four kids and a future I was looking forward too. Renee laughed, assuring me I was not overdosing. She told me to relax it would be okay. We left the party around two in the morning and everything still seemed to be moving so fast. When we arrived to my house, we decided that we were hungry. We made peanut butter and grape jelly sandwiches and ate them. We later tried to go to sleep and we just could not. We were wide awake. We sat in the kitchen for a while and then decided to clean up; there was nothing to clean up. Six in the morning came around and Renee suggested that we go to the laundry matt and do laundry. I thought that was a good idea and agreed. I told her I would go knock on my neighbor Peggy William's door to see if she wanted to go with us. I walked two houses down to her house and knocked on her door. She looked out of her upstairs bedroom window and said what are you doing out this early, and I told her I came to invite her to walk to the laundromat with Renee and me. Peggy said, "You are crazy, Lou! Wait for me I am going with you." We all went to the laundromat and did our laundry, washed and dried and returned home. Renee and I did not go to sleep until the early afternoon. That was the last time I ever swallowed a black beauty or any other pill that a doctor did not prescribe for me.

A few days later, we went to the Salvation Army to look for furniture. My kids and I did not need any clothing for our closets upstairs were not disturbed. Some others were not so fortunate. We found and old sofa and chair that was in good shape. We found a ride to get it to my house. About a month later, I had my sister's husband,

Rock; reupholster it in chocolate brown and red velvet material. It was beautiful when completed. I polished my coffee table, waxed that project flooring, purchased two lamps from Woolworth's, and now had an awesome living room. It was now time to bring my kids home from my mom's house since the house was livable. The only thing we were missing was a television in the living room but that was not a necessity at that time because we had a radio and a television in my bedroom. The grant money came in handy.

Next was the kitchen. I wanted to paint it, not the beige project housing color. Renee and I painted my fridge red and the walls black and silver in the kitchen. We thought it looked good. We did use the beige project housing color for the pantry. My mom walked down to my house not to long after we painted the kitchen and pantry.

Mom walked into the house and said, "Lord child, no one paints a kitchen black and silver." I told her I liked it. Mom said, "Sandra Lee you live here."

I just looked at her and smiled. It is now about the third week of July nineteen hundred and seventy two and I had not heard from Aaron for what seemed like forever. House phones were out and there were no cell phones or pagers in those days. I am looking forward to his call.

Chapter 28

I know where William Spent His time

THE SUMMER IS BLOOMING, AND everyone is out sporting his or her summer best. I just got off the phone talking to Aaron. We all survived the flood of Hurricane Agnes. He was well and said he would visit soon. I thought it was a great day to walk across the bridge to the east side to visit William's house where my sister Mary now lived. I gathered all of my kids, and we walked over the wooden College Avenue Bridge then through Penn Park to South Street. Mary was sitting on the front porch in a pair of shorts and a hair pick stuck in her afro. She had wire cutters in her hand, and I asked her just what was she going to do with the wire cutters? Mary mumbled through the wires in her mouth, and I could barely understand what she was saying. I asked her if she was cutting the wires in her mouth and she shook her head, yes. Mary had her mouth wired shut about a week or so before this day to help her lose weight. I told her she needed to try to hold on because there was no way she had lost any weight in a week or so. I helped her anyway to cut the wires out of her mouth. It was a messy task, but we got the wires out of her mouth. Tears were rolling down her face.

I asked her why she got the wires in if she was not going to stick with it.

She snapped back, "You try getting your mouth wired shut and can only have liquids through a straw."

I snapped back telling her not to be yelling at me, I did not have to help her fat-ass cut the wires out. I told her to go rinse her mouth out with salt water so she would not get an infection.

Mary stood up off the steps and said, "You might as well come inside, your sister is in the house."

I said, "Who?"

She said, "Come into the house and see."

Mary walked into the house first and my kids and I followed. There was a girl in the living room sitting and talking to William. She looked to be about my age. I did not know her, and she was not any girl that my mom, Dot Smallwood, brought into this world.

William looked at me and said, "You do not know who this is, do you?"

I responded, "Should I know who she is?"

Now William and I are talking as if the young woman was not present. We all three looked at each other. Mary was in the other room taking care of her mouth issues. William looked at me and said, "This is your sister Candy."

I was in some kind of indescribable thought, shock or something. I looked at Candy and said, "I apologize, I didn't know I had a sister named Candy."

Candy responded, "I knew about you and all of your sisters and your brother Bucky as well." I looked at her dead in the eyes to see if she looked like any of us. I introduced her to my kids.

Candy said to them, "I am your aunt Candace Washington. I live in Connecticut." I asked her how long she would be staying in York, Pennsylvania and she said for a few days then *Dad* was taking her back to Connecticut. At that moment, I invited her to walk with me to my house and William or Mary could come to get her later. Mary always had the keys to William's car. Mary yelled from the kitchen her dad can come for her. I could feel my sister Mary's feelings in her voice on that note. Mary was not feeling the half-sister news.

Candy and I had a lot to talk about that afternoon into the evening hours before she left. I asked her if I had any more siblings that I did not know about and she told me there were another sister and a brother, Barron and Talia. I met Talia that same summer. She came later to York to stay with William for several weeks. I invited Candy to return and stay with me for a few weeks along with her two daughters and her younger brother that she cared for.

The next morning, I walked to my mom's house about two to three blocks from me. I asked her if she knew that William had other children. She said she was aware that he did have other children. She told me that she knew of Candy and that she was not much older than I was. I told my mom that I invited her to come and stay with me for a few weeks. I asked my mom if that would bother her and she said no, it was up to me.

Candy returned to stay with me for a short stay in July-August after the Hurricane passed with her two little girls, Rhonda and Mona and her younger brother Bernard. Everyone in the neighbor soon knew I had a new half-sister. She and I discussed the ages of our siblings. Mary was nine months older than she was, she was nine months older than I was, Mabel one year younger than I was, Dottie Mae one year younger than Mabel was, Lugenia one year younger than Dottie Mae and Talia and Bonita about the same age. Wow, William was busy. There were bad vibes between my sister Bonita and Talia because Bonita was staying with William before Talia arrived. Remember, Bonita was the baby girl from my mom and dad. Candy and I were comfortable from the start. She was almost twenty-four and I was twenty-three. We hit it off just fine when we first met each other. We still hold our strong sister bond today. My mom told me not to be surprised if I found out that I had more brothers and sisters in York, Pennsylvania.

I said, "Mom, say it isn't so."

Mom looked at me and said, "I cannot say it is not so."

Now I know why William was missing in action at our house through most of my childhood years. Our father, William, had other outside families he was dealing with behind my mom's back. William, being a long-haul truck driver, had its rewards. Obviously, there were available women in all of the states where he traveled.

It was exciting to have this new older sister, Candy. I really liked her, and my mom embraced her. Not all of my siblings felt the same way. My mom was not feeling the other children that belonged to William, but only God knows that. Aaron called me the end of July, and I told him about my half-sister, Candace. Aaron knew about my sister Portia Owens from Baltimore. He had not met her yet. Portia's mom was my legal guardian while I was attending high school in Baltimore. I could not wait for Portia and Candace to meet each other and for them both to meet Aaron. I knew that they would all like each other for I loved all of them.

Chapter 29

Summer Is Slowing Down

I RECEIVED A CALL FROM AARON the first week in August, and he told me he would be coming in the following Friday evening. That was good because my sister Portia and her friend Kathy would be visiting that weekend, on that same Friday evening. Portia told me their arrival time so I phoned Doug and asked him if he could pick them up also. They would all be on the bus Aaron would be on from the Washington, DC. He said no problem. I described my sister and her friend to him. I phoned Portia after I finished the phone call with Doug and explained to her that Douglas Smallwood would be picking her and Kathy up at the bus terminal. I described him to her and told her to call from the payphone at the terminal if there were any problems when she arrived in York, Pennsylvania. It was already Sunday afternoon and Friday was only five days away. I needed to plan a little get-together for the weekend.

When Renee came home that early evening, I told her about everyone's visit on Friday and that we needed to throw a little house party on Saturday the following day. Renee told me she would take care of the beer and wine. I would take care of the food; Bonita volunteered to keep my kids on the weekend for a few dollars at her house. Her husband Barrion Banks was always cool with it. We were close, and I was his favorite sister in law. It's Friday and my kids and me are excited about Aaron's visit. The kids were always glad to see him because he always brought us all gifts, and we had not seen each other since the Hurricane Agnes Flood, for several weeks. Aaron, Portia, and Kathy were due in by 7:40 pm. I phoned Doug about 5:30 pm to make sure he had the time right and he told me to leave him alone, he got it. Bonita showed up about 7 pm for my kids and Tracey.

They arrived about 8:15 in the evening and when they entered my house, all of their faces seemed serious about something. I hugged them all and Portia said she had to go to the bathroom. I told her and Kathy to come upstairs so I could show them the sleeping arrangements. When we got upstairs, Portia did not have to go to the bathroom. She wanted to tell me about her and Kathy's encounter with Aaron when they got on the bus in Baltimore.

"That little slant-eyed, yellow man thinking he was cute or something. He did not even speak to us when we slid in our seats across from him. He acted as if he did not hear us speak to him. That was not even half of it. When we walked out getting our luggage, he did not look for any luggage. He grabbed his little shoulder bag, spotted and walked over to your cousin Doug, and said, "My man." They gave each other the dap handshake, and I heard him say let's go. I knew that was your cousin from the description you gave me, and he called him Doug. Doug told him he was picking up two other people. The two females who sat across from me on the bus. We all greeted each other and got in the car. His yellow ass got in the front seat and only held a conversation with Doug. I was too through when he got out of the car at your house."

Portia asked me if that was the awesome Air Force guy I told her about, and I confirmed it with a big smile on my face. Portia said,

"Damn!" She, Kathy, and I laughed about it. I showed them to the rooms where they would be sleeping, and Aaron already knew his way to my room. He did not need an escort. When they settled down, we went downstairs, and I officially introduced them all. Doug said his goodbyes because he had to go home. He said he told his wife, Yvette, that he was going to pick up Aaron for me and drop him off at my house.

He said, "You know cuz, Yvette can tell time and she knows about how long it would take me."

I said, "I guess you had better take your ass home then." We all laughed. I told him if you are not busy tomorrow, stop by for food, drinks, and card playing.

It was now after nine in the evening, and we sat around talking and drinking wine. Aaron pulled out a joint and started smoking it. Just about then, Rene showed up and asked, "Who got the weed?" Aaron pulled out another already rolled up joint and gave it to her. I was so dumb, I asked them what kind of cigarettes they were smoking, and Aaron and Renee laughed. I did not even smoke cigarettes and never did start. Portia and Kathy did not partake and continued to sip their wine. About 12:45 am, we were all ready to sleep. We all went to our sleeping areas after I locked up the house, doors and windows. The only house alarm in the projects was one's eyes and ears or the eyes and ears of their neighbor.

Aaron and I continued to have our wine in my bedroom; he wanted to tell me about his bus ordeal. He pulled out the gifts for the kids, got undressed and jumped into my warm bed to join me. I told him what Portia said to me about the bus trip.

Aaron said to me, "Wait a minute let me tell you about your sister and her friend. When they got on the bus, they were so loud, as if they wanted some attention. They walked down the aisle and sat directly across from me. The bus was not crowded, they could have chosen another seat if they were uncomfortable sitting next to me. I noticed them, they were fine sisters, but I was not interested in them. They had my attention when they boarded the bus. They were too damn loud, and I was not looking for anyone. I knew the woman I was going to see, and she was not a loud mouth. I took out my cassette and headphones and listened to some jazz. When we all got into the car, I just kept my conversation with your cousin. We arrived at your house and they got out, grabbed their bags, and started through your backyard. I started thinking have they been here before. I thought to myself, *they are not with Doug.* Sandra when you told me that was your sister and her friend down in the kitchen, I was glad I did not say anything to them on the bus or on the ride here. They were both fine, it could have went a different way, but I am only interested in you."

The next morning Aaron and I woke up very early, about 5 am. That was early for me. He said it was routine. He awakened in the morning on the Air Force Base early every morning. It gave him enough time to make it to the mess hall for breakfast before reporting to his duty station. I asked what the mess hall was, and he explained it was the dining room where his meals were free. I told him that I had breakfast food but not enough for all of us. He walked to the corner store and got some breakfast food. I offered to pay, but he would not take it. When he returned, he helped me to cook and we placed all food in the oven so Portia, Renee, and Kathy could help themselves when they were ready to eat -- scrambled eggs, fried potatoes, sausage, and bacon. Everyone woke up in a reasonable time except my sister Portia who always slept to one in the afternoon when we were teens. I guess she still had that habit from our school days. When she did eventually wake up, she helped herself to the now cold food. There were no microwave ovens back in those days, so she just took out a pan and heated the rest of the food and sat down and ate her breakfast. It was going to be a busy day. We had a card party to get ready for in the evening.

My house was the "Do-Drop-In." My friends, cousins, neighbors in and out all day. Renee left the house early afternoon to go to the liquor store to get the beer and wine for the card party.

When she returned, Aaron asked her where the hard liquor was.

Renee responded, "Do you have money for that?" In addition, he said, "How much do you need?" Renee looked across the room (we were all in the kitchen, the hang out place) to me and I tilted my head up, eye-to-eye contact. She tilted her head down and said to Aaron "Fifty should do it." Renee did not drive but knew everybody and anybody she needed to know to get things done. She was off again and returned later, much later, with the hard liquor. It was time to get the party started.

York, Pennsylvania was a small place back then. The knocks on the door continued all evening into the night. People were playing cards and others were just drinking in the living room having good conversations. Bucky Branch, Tiny, Sam Watson, Wayne Bailey, Wendell Murry, and there are too many others to remember. About nine pm, Doug showed up and started everyone playing Bullshit. I had never heard of that game nor did my friends. It was fun. You had to swallow from the liquor bottle if you were slow in responding. I was not a real drinker at all but played the game. (I did not drink anything stronger than wine and I did not play cards, so why should I participate in a game with liquor included? There had to be a better way to entertain friends.) It was now two o'clock in the morning and time for all who was not staying at my house to get out. Renee kicked everyone out for me. All was now quiet for the rest of the night. However, comes morning, all of that drinking was a mistake. I was so sick the next morning. No more bullshit games for me.

Sunday morning about 8 am, my baby girl Karmentrina was calling me on the phone with the help of her aunt Bonita. She wanted to know if they could come home now so they could see Aunt Portia and Aaron. I told her yes and Aaron and I walked the few blocks to my sister's house to get my kids. Thanked my sister and grabbed my kids and walked back home where everyone was still asleep. My kids were all happy to see Aaron; Kimmy Jo was still skeptical about Aaron. Keenan Wynn wanted Aaron to carry him on his back and he did. Karmentrina was a little jealous so I had Aaron carry Keenen Wynn half way and then carry Karmentrina the rest of the way home. We reached our house soon, and I know Aaron was glad to see the door.

He went to my room, called the kids upstairs, and gave them all envelopes with a five-dollar bill in it. I told him on previous occasions that he could not give them a lot of money. Kevin Scott wanted to know if they could all walk around the corner to the neighborhood store. I told him they had to save it until tomorrow. His little glasses steamed up from crying because he wanted to spend that money and not the next day. I needed to teach them how to hold on to their money. My ten-year-old niece Tracey was okay with it. She was at the age where she knew that amount was not a big deal. Early afternoon everyone was now up; Portia and Kathy had to catch an early bus. Aaron was taking that same bus. They all knew each other now. The travel should be a much better relaxing trip back to Baltimore, Maryland and Washington, DC. When Portia arrived home, she called me to let me know they arrived safely. Portia also told me that she thought Aaron was a nice person and all he talked about on the bus was my kids and me.

No sooner than Portia, Kathy, and Aaron left, Candace called me on the phone to see if she, her two daughters, and her bother Bernard could come to stay for the weekend this coming Friday. I told her no problem. Aaron was now coming to see the kids and me weekly on weekends. I gave him a key to the house on his last visit. He had not met my sister Candy yet, but he would see her soon. Sure enough, on Friday early afternoon, she arrived at my back-kitchen doorstep with our dad, William, her brother Bernard and her daughters. The last time Candy and I hung out so much at the American Legion and the Elks. This next time we made our way through York, The American Legion with live bands, The Elks Lodge, Speak Easy's, house parties, outside festivals, you name it we were there. After a week of hanging out, all the local young men in the area knew, there was a new girl at my house. I already had my share of friends coming in and out on a regular. Now they were looking for Candy. She told me one morning Harold Lewter was picking her up to hang out. I guess Candy knew her way around now. The weekend would be no problem, for she now knew many people.

That Friday about 12 midnight, Aaron showed up with one of his military friends, Paige. Paige drove him to York. It was so late. Aaron did not knock on the door; he used his own door key. According to him, he walked in and saw what he thought was me sleeping on the living room couch waiting for him. He was mistaken; it was Candy. He ran his hand up her pajama gown.

I heard her scream, "Who in the hell are you?"

I hear him respond, "Who in the hell are you? I thought you were Sandra, my woman!"

Candy said, "Your woman Sandra is upstairs in her room asleep! I am her sister Candace."

Aaron replied, I met all of her sisters and brothers not long ago at her mom's house. Sandra never mentioned you."

Candy said, "Allow me to introduce myself. My name is Candace Washington, and I am Sandra's half-sister. We share a father." I think I remember her telling me something about a half-sister.

He answered and said, "I am Aaron Edward Paul Stockton, and I am your sister's man." I was in the stairwell enjoying their conversation.

I turned on the light, walked into the living room, and said, "I guess you both know each other now." I now had to make sleeping arrangements for Paige. I instructed Candace to go to my room and I gave Aaron and Paige blankets and pillows and told them to pretend they were in the field somewhere. We all laughed. Well the weekend for Candace and her family's visit went quick. She visited back and forth from Bridgeport, Connecticut from then on. One big happy family we were.

September and a new school year had started. My being an advocate with Caroline Sexton to defend others less fortunate then ourselves was most gratifying, but I knew that the merry-go-round that I had been on since Joseph's Death had to stop somewhere where there would be permanence and security for my children and me. Soon after Labor Day when I received a call from Aaron, I told him my plan of needing stability, and I wanted to know his plan. I asked him if he had any plans on marrying my children and me in the future.

He told me, and in these exact works, "I have not thought about it, and I think I am not ready for such a responsibility."

I told Aaron in my most caring voice, that I did truly understand and that I would continue to see him as we are now, but I would be looking.

He said to me, "What does that mean Sandra?"

"Aaron, that means that I will do whatever I have to do to find a husband for me and a father for my children. All of them to include Kimmy Jo, Kevin Scott, Karmentrina Schevelle, Keenan Wynn and my niece Tracey."

Aaron was quiet on his end and repeated he needed some time to think about it; I answered: "I will wait for your call."

At that point, I knew as time went on and I grew, developed, and changed daily that everything and everyone in my circle of life would have to respond accordingly. I decided I would wait for Aaron's response but not too long. I had to continue to thrive positively; however, that may have been with him or my next knight in shining armor. I sure hoped that phone would ring and I would hear the right answer from the other side.

THE END

Reflections

Gerald (Gerri) Wright (A Codorus Street Resident of the 1950s and 1960s era)

Excerpt from the First Annual Codorus Street Reunion Booklet at Martin Luther King Jr. Park York, Pennsylvania. July 28, 2012.

I WANT TO SHARE WITH THE descendants of the Codorus Street families that during our time, there were no gangs, minimum drug use, and rare shootings. Let us honor our ancestors and their vision that they had for our futures. Their vision was that if you worked hard and got a good education the sky was the limit. All across Northern America, African American families migrated from the Southern States to the Northern States to provide their children with opportunities deprived of in the South. They endured the humiliation and indigenous?? of segregation to afford their families a better life in the urban cities. Codorus Street was an integrated street, one of those settlement cities in York, Pennsylvania. However, a system called block busting, eventually turned the street into an all-Black Ghetto. Prior to this time, Black and White neighbors lived harmoniously. Codorus Street was just one block long, bordered by Penn Street, Green Street, College Avenue, and the Codorus Creek. Our kind, trusting, Christian parents were not sophisticated enough to recognize the manipulation of "Big City" power structure and the imminent domain manipulation that caused the demolition of our homes.

Codorus Street was a happy place for all of us until urban renewal came through and changed our lives forever. The last family moved off the block in 1961. It was an end to an era when the culture of "it takes a village to raise a child" was a big part of our community. The Proverb "It Takes a Village" originates from the Nigerian Igbo culture that meant that the child did not belong to one parent or one home, regardless of the biological parents. There were several streets/communities in York City, Pennsylvania that met the same urban renewal fate as the Codorus Street families in 1950s and the 1960s.

I feel that if our ancestors were here today to see what we have accomplished, they would be proud and tell us to carry on because the struggle is not over for the African American People.

Thanks for taking a walk down memory lane with me.

Respectfully, Gerri Wright.

Ruth Anne Minor, Retired Lieutenant Colonel US Army Nurse Corp. February 27, 2019, Spotsylvania, Virginia.

It was a very hot summer day in San Antonio, Texas June 1992. New soldiers from all over the United Sates and OCONUS were arriving for the Army Officers Advanced Military Course. I noticed Sandra sitting alone in the classroom. She looked a little older than the soldiers I was seeing there, so far. I walked over to her and said, you look about my age, (I was greater than 10 years older than she was, or so I thought). We can collaborate to survive this course.

I said where are the Black Officers are hiding? Scanning and looking around there were about 8-10 in the class of over 100 whites, mostly young white arrogant ROTC students that were getting on my last nerve. It looked as though we had an all-White Cadre too. I was thinking that we few black officers were going to catch hell. Sandra just looked up at me and smiled. She reached her hand out to me and said, hello, I am Captain Stockton from Maryland. I smiled and said I am from Spotsylvania, Virginia. I sat down beside her. I told her that I was not for any prejudicial games; I was not drafted for any bullshit. I do not owe the government/military anything. I volunteered for this I can quit.

Sandra looked at me, smiled and said, "No you cannot, you signed a contract. I got your back." We will make it through this course. THEY need US to train THEM." A comfortable feeling surrounded me and my anxiety faded, she made sure I understood that we as Strong Black Women are used to challenges and struggles and this training was just a ripple in the pond. Through the weeks, months, years that followed, greater than 16, with her encouragement, and 'go get it' positive attitude, I retired as a Lieutenant Colonel. She mentored many soldiers, enlisted and officers in their career tracks. I can only describe Sandra as Candid, Sharp, and Fearless. If you crossed her...she kept quiet, but her face spoke to you loud and clear.

The most remarkable was her sacrifices she gave for her children to be successful. The biological mother of four as well as the foster mother of over 100 or greater children.

A poor Black child form the inner city of York, Pennsylvania, that had self-esteem to recognize her worth to fight to improve her situation thru education and hard work. To not only benefit herself but to benefit her prodigy and those who have come under her tutelage. As I watched and listened when I first met her and the struggles she had undergone in order to succeed in her endeavors, it is with admiration, pride and comment commitment? to a friendship that is everlasting through the test of time.

A strong woman, not ego driven, she loves, and cares for so many; today she is still giving and sharing. Family and friends address her as the Matriarch.

Marion Peterson Fields - A Lifetime Friendship. (Cookie) March 26, 2020), Alliance, North Carolina.

Our lifelong friendship seemed to have developed from our "nerdyness" A need to acquire the life we both wanted. Lou affectionately known as Sandra Lee Smallwood would be the one person who understood me. Lou's house was full of females, six girls, and one boy. Her sisters gave me a firsthand experience of a sisterhood between sisters. This was a treasured experience for me. My house on the other hand was full of males. I was the only girl of five children. The need to define ourselves for ourselves. Studies did that. I remember doing homework at Lou's house that was a very busy place in contrast to my house, which was full of male chaos. Having females around me gave me a sense of belonging, which I could not get at home. Lou's voice always carried a kind of authority with her sisters and her brother. They would fuss back but Lou's word would always win out. Male dominance won out in my house. My only escape was to my lonely room.

I gravitated to Lou because of her straight forwardness, lion heartedness, and pointedly honest. We hit it off famously. We shared that. "Don't ask if you don't want to know", attitude. Our conversations covered anything that concerned black girl teen aged angst!" Even when we could not hang out like we used to always do because of situations and life changing occurrences, where we did have the chances, laughs, and talks of "how we handled" that. That was the crux of the cement of our lasting friendship. Even now, I marvel at those times when "girlfriend oil" lubricated our lasting friendship, rather "Sister Queen" close relationship.

Growing up in York, County of York Pennsylvania, the Friday night hops at the YWCA and hanging out at the Old Crispus Attucks were the places to be. My Mother had many other activities for my brothers and me to do. Cub scouts, girl scouts, and any other activity she could think of to keep us busy. My Mom's motto was "My kids will not be given to the streets but to the Church." Shiloh Baptist Church was our home away from home. My life was very structured. Every chance I got to escape I did to Lou's house. Lou's Mom and her sisters opened my mind to the world, as teens would have it back then. Only when my relationship with my mom went south did I declare my freedom and learn of the other side of being a "wild child." I had a job working at the Yorktown Hotel before and after school. When I had free time I was at Lou's house, chatting endless girl stuff or hanging out with her and Joe Kearse as well as her sisters. Miss Dot, her mom, allowed me to stay at their house when things were crazy at my house. She told me I had to go to work and school like I always did when I was at home. My Mom was ok with me being at Miss Dot's house with Lou. Miss Dot was the mom to many children, not just hers. I found out later that Miss Dot spoke with my mom about me staying at her house. My mom was grateful for she didn't want me out in the community somewhere with no supervision.

As time went on, we all were growing up and having less time to spend with each other. I was getting my own place and working hard to keep everything together. My brother Lafayette (Bink) and Lou became very good friends. He would bring homework for her from school when she was expecting Kimmy Jo her first child. They had some of the same classes in the tenth grade. It would not be long before she moved to Baltimore, Maryland. Our friendship has lasted theses fifty years plus. Though having lost touch through the years, the friendship never ceases from remaining intact. Social media has given much to staying in contact with the ones we love.

A York Pennsylvania Local Newspaper Article.

Article written by Bruce W. Pringle 1972

Vocalist Sandi Kearse looked at Al Johnson (Rest in Peace) like a weary private might eye a harsh drill sergeant. "All you want to do tonight is scream at us, "she told Johnson, manager of the ten members York Based Rock group, Freedom Pride. Johnson whose professional music experience dates back to days on the sound circuit with York's legendary R&B group the, Quinone's, listened with the patience of a soldier who has been around long enough to expect gripes from his troops. "I guess you are right," he answered "but that is my job." Moreover, with that being said, he returned to the task – criticizing the group's performance at a recent performance.

HARD TO FAULT – Actually, his criticisms were few. It was understandably difficult for him to find fault with a show that contained only a limited number of miscues Freedoms Pride had come on stage before a ballroom gathering at the Yorktown Hotel of stylish young adults who sat at neatly adorned tables of eight politely sipping overpriced drinks. By the time they finished their soul oriented show, many of the tables were empty and the drinks forsaken, as hundreds of persons erupted to fill the dance floor. Clearly, the group had scored a major success.

Yet Johnson was not satisfied. Sandi, he said had appeared almost stern and Tam Kennedy and Ted Ritter had not varied the choreography enough and some of the between songs, instrumental needed improvement. Sandi, who is quick to say, she really does not mind Johnsons criticism and asserts, "Al is not afraid to tell us when we goof even if he is talking about something minor we know that he is trying to help us."

Drummer Willie Williams agrees. "He pushes us really hard." Willie says the results are worth all of the yelling. The results thus far include an appearance with Jerry Butler, one of pop music's most respected vocalists. Financial backing by a local booking agency and several recording offers, and a reputation as one of York's most potent rockers. Besides Sandi, Tam and Ted and Willie on drums, Freedoms Pride organized last November, includes, Linda Dowling also on vocals. Jeff Murphy lead guitar, Blaine Weisser, bass guitar, Brian Silverman, organ, Janet Zutell, trumpet and Kirt Zutell, reed instruments. Willie age 24 is the oldest member of the group while Kirt 15, id the youngest member of the group.

The group's current goal is to assemble music and choreography for a nightclub act, consisting of five completely different one-hour routines. "We have about three hours of material together now," Johnson says, "but we do not want to go out on the road fulltime until we are sure we are ready." Too many regular patrons of local nightclubs, Freedoms Pride may seem to be setting their sights rather high. Few groups who play this area are reluctant to perform the same song two or three times during their act. Few, choreographed at all and perhaps most important, few demonstrate the expertise already exhibited by Freedom's Pride.

Kimmy Jo Kearse, CD Title "I GIVE YOU ME."

Lyrics to a song my daughter dedicated to me on her first solo compact disc in 2004

(A Song for Mom)

Will I ever be like you?
Will I do the things you do?
Will I ever have the strength that you've shown me?
You love us all with your heart.
Loved us all right from the start.
Mom--- Will I ever be like you?

You're always there for all our needs
We can all depend on you.
What would happen if you weren't here for me?
What would I be? What would I do without you?

I Wonder

Will I ever be like you?
Have all the things you do?
Not the material things, but what you possess inside.
I'm proud to have you on my side
I know in you I can confide.
But Mom----Will I ever be like you?

You're such an inspiration
You mean so much to me
I'll know I've finally made it
If I turn out to be-------Like you (hold note)

Will I ever be like you?
Will I do the things you do?
Will I ever have the strength that you've shown me?
You love us all with your heart.
Loved us all right from the start.
Mom--- Will I ever be like you?

A Letter from Sandra addressed to her dead husband, six months after his death. Sandra Felt it helped her to grieve her loss and move on with her life. December 22, 1969

Dear Joseph ;

Although you are gone from this earth — you arn't really gone or you'll never be gone from my heart. Dearest Joseph I'll always love you forever and forever more. I know now not to ask GOD why he took you from me and the children, for he has an unknown answer. I often wonder how you are resting , strange as it seems I do wonder about you. I talk to you day in and day out because I can't seem to understand why! THINGS HAVE TO BE THIS WAY!

Joseph I loved you as my boyfriend, I LOVED YOU AS MY HUSBAND, and I can and will love you as my BROTHER when I'm dead and gone from this earth. I would like to be right beside you just like it used to be. Our DAUGHTER Kimmy Jo always does asked about , Kevin Scott does also and if Karmentrina were much older than 3 months of age she would of course , have remembered you. (YOU ARE THE LOVEABLE TYPE) WE LOVE YOU SO VERY MUCH — I'll keep right on telling them that you are just resting and that we'll see you soon — GOD is ready for us to join you. (when he calls)

JOE the last time you and I talked it was a beautiful thing and after you left I TALKED TO GOD AND HE TOLD ME THAT IT WILL BE SOON WHEN YOU'LL BE BACK TO TALK TO ME AGAIN! I trust in GOD and I always will as long as I live no matter what any-one says. God be with you until then and abide with you forever and forever more, I'll always think about you .

GOD BE WITH YOU AT ALL TIMES,
Mrs. Joseph Kearse (Sandra Kearse)

December 22, 1969
P.S. Joseph always remember that the man
who shot you will pay the price for
his sin— he will always be bothered
by your reflections!

1

204

Persons in my life who have influenced Permanent, Positive changes in me.

My Mother, Dorothy Mae Jackson -Smallwood (11/27/1927-2/01/1992), My Father, William Junior Smallwood (01/11/1921), My Sister, Dorothy Mae Smallwood-Stewart (Midget) (07/23/1951-02/01/1992), My Brother, Clifford Earl Smallwood "Bucky" (09/25/1955), My Guardian Mother, Bernice Alene Owens (12/28/1928-10/30/1995), My Guardian Brother, James A. Owens (08/09/1954-11/25/2006, and sister Portia Owens. My Step-Father, William Henry Duncan (Mr. Bill – 04/01/1918), My Paternal Grandmother, Mabel Paul-Smallwood (08/26/1902, My Husband Joseph Kearse (04/10/1947), My Sister-in-Law Cressie Kearse (08/10/1949-03/16/2004), My Maternal Grandmother, Margaret Ryan Jackson-McGee (08/08/1908-03/29/1966), My Maternal Grandfather, Charles Jackson (08/05/1902-06/14/1967), One of my very closest Girlfriends, Joanne Clayton-Borders (09/11/1945-09/24/2012, One of my favorite first cousins, William Lee Smallwood (07/02/1945-01/30/2019 and My Loving Aunt, Vera Horton-Smallwood (05/26/1926-03/21/2019. My Maternal Aunt Joanne McGee-Grant, Mt Paternal Aunt "Sis' Lugenia Smallwood-Miller (04/28/2003), My Maternal Uncle Charles McGee, Aaron Edward Stockton. My Maternal Aunt Almeda Jackson (1924-1991).

Never underestimate your own ability to affect positive change in others. We are stronger together.

A big thank you to Jeffrey Kirkland, Historian, York, Pennsylvania, Ruth Anne Minor, Retired Lieutenant Colonel, USA, Sharon Singleton, Retired Colonel USA, Portia Owens-Perry, Marion Paterson-Fields of North Carolina, Mary Richardson York, Pennsylvania, Geraldine Wright York Pennsylvania, Douglas Smallwood Sr., and Corretta Doctorr without her this book may not have been written.

Photos

Bonita and Clifford

Dottie Mae Smallwood younger sister

Joe Kearse and Sandra Prom 1968

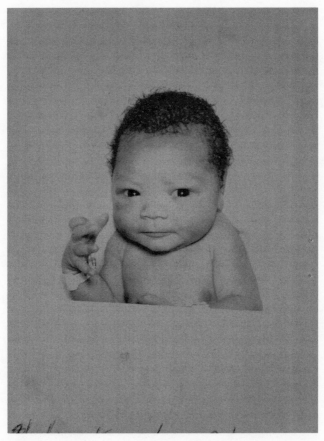

Karmentrina born when I was in 12th grade

Karmentrina and Keenan in Phila. Pa.

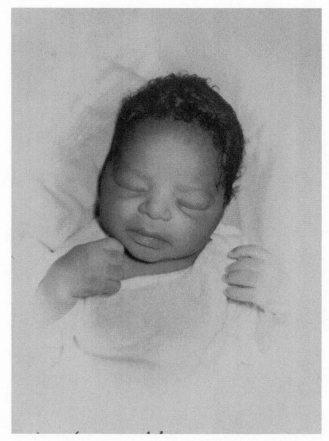

4ᵗʰ child Keenan Wynn-denied by his father

Kimmy Jo and Kevin in Phia. Pa.

Kimmy Jo, Kevin Scott, Tracey, Karmentrina and Keenan Wynn

Mabel Smallwood (sister) and Sandra Flood of Hurricane Agnes

Margaret Ryan Jackson–McGee Maternal Grandmother

Sandra and her mother, Dorothy Mae Jackson

Bottom row, Mom (Dorothy), Dottie Mae, Lugenia
Middle –Mary, Bonita, Mabel
Top Row Clifford, Sandra, Dad (William)